Dario Fo is a leading light of anti-establishm... theatre in Italy. His plays translated into English include *Accidental Death of an Anarchist, Can't Pay? Won't Pay!* and *Female Parts* (written with Franca Rame). His international reputation continues to grow – his most recent triumph was at 1984 Edinburgh Festival fringe.

Dario Fo

Trumpets and Raspberries

Edited by Franca Rame

Translated and adapted
by R. C. McAvoy and A.-M. Giugni
Introduction by Stuart Hood

Pluto Plays

English translation first published in 1984 by Pluto Press Ltd,
The Works, 105a Torriano Avenue, London NW5 2RX and Pluto Press
Australia Limited, PO Box 199, Leichhardt, New South Wales 2040,
Australia

ISBN 0 86104 6765

Phototypeset by AKM Associates (UK) Limited,
Ajmal House, Hayes Road, Southall, London
Printed by Photobooks (Bristol) Limited
Bound by W.H. Ware & Sons Limited
Tweed Road, Clevedon, Avon

Contents

The Pola Jones production of *Trumpets and Raspberries* opened at the Palace Theatre, Watford on October 4 and transferred to the Phoenix Theatre, London on November 15 1984.

CAST (In order of appearance)

Orderly 1	**Robbie Barnett**
Orderly 2	**John Levitt**
Orderly 3	**Gavin Muir**
Orderly 4	**Simon Williamson**
Doctor	**Christopher Ettridge**
Rosa Berardi	**Gwen Taylor**
Antonio Berardi	**Griff Rhys Jones**
Lucia	**Francesca Brill***
Agnelli	**Griff Rhys Jones**
Inspector	**Jeffrey Chiswick**
Examining Magistrate	**John Levitt**
Policeman	**Gavin Muir**
Group Leader	**Christopher Ettridge**
Secret Agent 1	**Robbie Barnett**
Secret Agent 2	**Simon Williamson**
Man with Dishwasher	**Gavin Muir**

Directed by	**Roger Smith**
Designed by	**Fran Thompson**
Lighting by	**Mick Hughes**

ACT I
Scene 1 The recovery room in the Agnelli Foundation Hospital
Scene 2 The same, some months later.

INTERVAL

ACT II
Scene 1 The living room of Rosa Berardi's apartment in Turin
Scene 2 The same a few weeks later.

*During the run at the Palace Theatre, Lucia was played by Celia Montague

Introduction

by Stuart Hood

The plot of *Trumpets and Raspberries* is based on a simple assumption. It is that Agnelli, the powerful head of the Fiat Motor Corporation, has been kidnapped, unwittingly rescued by a Communist shop steward from the Fiat works, but badly disfigured in the process. This leads to a hopeless confusion of identities between Agnelli and the shop steward – a confusion which baffles his wife, his girlfriend and the police. As in much of Fo's work, the strength of the piece comes from the tension between the farcical situations in which the characters find themselves and the background of political mayhem in Italian society.

It is easy to see where Fo got the idea for the kidnapping. When the play was first performed in 1981 the abduction by the Red Brigades of the Christian Democrat politician, Aldo Moro, and his subsequent murder was in everyone's minds – as was the suspicion that his colleagues in the government might have saved him had they tried a little harder. The kidnapping took place at a time in the 1970s when the Christian Democrats were playing 'the politics of tension', working up a state of panic about terrorism which allowed the introduction of special measures aimed not only at the Red Brigades but at all the forces to the left of the Communist Party. (Right-wing terrorism, in which the secret services probably had a hand, was less vigorously prosecuted.) It was a time, too, when the Italian Communist Party had embarked on the policy of 'historical compromise' with the Christian Democrats and claimed the right to play its part in running the state. It became a strong supporter of law and order. The political conformism of the Party is reflected in the behaviour of the shop steward, who is submissive to authority and much less able to cope than his wife or girlfriend.

Why Agnelli? Because he was not only the head of Fiat but also chairman of Confindustria, the equivalent of the Confederation of British Industries. He also ruled over a great financial empire with tentacles in many sectors of Italian life and huge investments abroad – including Poland and the Soviet Union, both of which have Fiat factories. His programme was the same as Ian MacGregor's of the National Coal Board: to rationalise, to introduce automation, to cut back the work force and to destroy the power of the unions on the shopfloor. The fact that, in the play, he is rescued by one of his own shop stewards is therefore specially ironical.

Agnelli was also an important political figure – a man who believed in the 'strong state' and was suspected of being involved along with dubious figures from the extreme Right in manoeuvres to overthrow the government. But paradoxically he also believed that one solution to the Italian situation was an alliance between industry and the Italian Communist Party to run the country efficiently.

The reaction of the Fiat workers to Agnelli's policies was demonstrations against 'the policy of sacrifice' in the streets and factories, where trade union officials who collaborated were paraded through the plants. It was a time when the workers turned away from the Communist Party to other forces on the Left, which included Maoists – the shop steward's girlfriend is a Maoist – and other loosely organised groups. In 1977 there was a great police sweep leading to mass arrests and the imprisonment of thousands of suspects, some of whom are still awaiting trial. Thanks to the evidence of 'super-grasses' like those used by the British in Northern Ireland, a large number of people were put on trial or held in special prisons where inhuman conditions led to riots that were suppressed with great violence.

At the end of one of the first performances of this play relatives of some of these prisoners came on stage and requested to read a document inviting doctors and journalists to visit the worst and see with their own eyes how impossible conditions were. Fo's wife, the actress Franca Rame, had been active in drawing the attention of Amnesty International to the plight of these prisoners. She had also supported Soccorso Rosso (Red Aid), an organisation to help prisoners and their families. This incident led to an extraordinary campaign against Fo and Rame, accusing them of supporting the Red Brigades although they have made clear their disapproval of terrorism as a political weapon. It was a campaign which spread into parliament where a Social Democrat senator and a Communist senator joined in, calling for legal proceedings against the couple. It was, as Dario Fo has said, 'a sand-storm' raised by the authorities in an attempt to confuse and disorientate the public.

The laughter, the political jokes of *Trumpets and Raspberries*, were an intervention in Italian politics at a moment when there were more political prisoners in Italy than there had been under Fascism. Like Fo's other political farces it is on an important level a serious play. Laughter, says Franca Rame, opens not only people's mouths but their minds as well and allows some shafts of reason to strike home.

Stuart Hood
September 1984

Characters

Antonio Berardi/Gianni Agnelli
Lucia Rismondi
Rosa Berardi
Doctor/Secret Agent
1st Ward Orderly/1st Secret Agent
2nd Ward Orderly/2nd Secret Agent
3rd Ward Orderly/3rd Secret Agent
4th Ward Orderly/4th Secret Agent
Examining Magistrate/Man with dishwasher

ACT 1

Scene 1

The stage lights come up slowly. We find ourselves in the recovery ward of a hospital. Four hospital ORDERLIES bustle about. They are wearing operating-theatre gear – green gowns, green caps, plastic gloves and clown-like antiseptic masks. As the lights come up, the WARD ORDERLIES are bringing equipment on stage – various bits of electronic apparatus, and two office-style chairs on castors. Everything is covered with sheets of transparent cellophane, to indicate that the place is kept scrupulously germ-free.

One of the ORDERLIES arranges a very large and conspicuous bust of a man. This is mounted on a silver pedestal, and it too is wrapped in cellophane.

From the rear of the stage, enter the DOCTOR and ROSA MINELLI.

Doctor This way, please, madam . . . we just want you to identify the patient.
Rosa (*Almost bumping into the bust*) Oh, that's not him.
Doctor This is a statue of Agnelli.[1] Our whole Recovery Ward was funded by the Agnelli Foundation.
Rosa I thought that was the patient!

A WARD ORDERLY offers ROSA a theatre gown to put on.

Do I have to put it on?
Orderly Of course, madam.
Doctor Madam, if you don't feel up to it, we could postpone it till later.
Rosa No, no . . . I want to see him straight away. I'm ready . . .
Doctor Yes indeed, he looks pretty awful, even for us, and we should be used to it. He's completely disfigured you know.
Rosa Disfigured? (*Starting to cry*) Oh God . . . Poor Antonio . . .

The ORDERLY slips a pair of canvas hospital over-shoes onto her feet.

Rosa What are you doing? (*Speaking normally*) Ah, is it for the polishing? Are you short staffed? Oh all right, I don't mind. Disfigured eh? And to think, he had such a handsome face . . . So open and likeable . . . You won't believe this, Professor, but I still loved him, even if he really didn't deserve it . . . when you think of the way he's treated me . . .
Doctor She's getting overwrought. Prepare me a suppository with twenty drops of Asvanol Complex . . .
Rosa Don't bother, Professor . . . I won't need it . . . I've already told you . . . I have no feelings for him . . . To me, my husband . . . was like a stranger . . . I haven't seen him for months. I can cope.
Doctor I believe you . . . but it's just a precaution you know. I don't want to risk

provoking a trauma in you, but it's for the identification . . . Unfortunately, the law requires it. Now come along madam, and be strong.

At a signal from the DOCTOR, *a mobile stretcher-bed is wheeled onstage. Lying on it is the body of* ROSA'S *presumed husband,* ANTONIO. *In fact it is a dummy, which is all bandaged up and in plaster. The* WARD ORDERLIES *take the ends of the wires which hang down from an overhead frame, and connect them to the dummy's extremities. In this way, as occasion demands, he can be made to move like a large string puppet. The dummy's entry is accompanied by a musical interlude.*

ROSA *gets up and speaks to the dummy.*

Rosa Oh my God, Antonio, what have they done to you?! (*She faints, and is held up by the* DOCTOR *and one of the* ORDERLIES)

Doctor Come on, come on . . . Be brave . . . Breathe deeply.

Rosa His nose . . . He hasn't got a nose any longer . . . It's all mashed to a pulp! And he already had sinusitis! And his chin . . . That's gone too. Let me near him!

Doctor (*To the* ORDERLIES) No, keep her away!

Rosa They've obliterated my Antonio . . . There's nothing left of him . . . apart from his ears. Antonio, Antonio! You see? He's got two ears, but he doesn't hear me!

Doctor Obviously . . . He's in a deep coma.

Rosa Oh, he's lost weight. It's that girl he's taken up with, the one who stole him away from me! Do you realise, she had him going out jogging?! Just imagine, a man of his age, a worker, admittedly a skilled worker . . . You force him to go running in a red tracksuit with 'Parmalat' written all over the back . . . a pom-pom hat with 'Michelin' stamped all over it, and 'Marlboro' track shoes . . . By the end, he looked more like a racing Ferrari . . . !

Doctor Hurry up with that suppository, and please prepare me a syringe with Mecardizol.

Rosa Don't bother about the hypodermic . . . If it's for me, at the very least I'll end up with an abscess on my backside! And then they have the nerve to talk about crime waves and terrorism . . . What about Agnelli? Those bastard managers at Fiat . . . with Agnelli at their head! They sent him to service some generator, hanging God knows how many feet up in the air, without safety gear . . . One careless moment and splat! A triple somersault with no safety net!

Doctor No, madam, the accident didn't happen at the Circus[2] . . . I mean, in the factory, at Fiat.

Rosa Oh no? And how can you be so sure? . . . Were you there?

Doctor No, but the hospital almoner's department looked into it. They made some brief inquiries. Yesterday, your husband was absent from work all afternoon.

Rosa But where can it have happened, then?

Doctor Maybe he was knocked down by a car . . . Some hit and run driver. In fact the person who handed him over to the Red Cross promptly – poof – disappeared!

Rosa Poof was he aye?May God strike him down! May he give him a dose of St Vitus' Dance, and gonorrhea, so that when he gets the shakes his whatsits drop off! Oh, Antonio, if only you'd stayed with me . . . I bet they ran you over while you were out jogging! It's all the fault of that bitch . . . Don't get me wrong, Professor . . . She's a good-looking girl, but beauty's only skin deep and any woman of 23 can take a man's fancy . . . She makes me laugh! You should have seen – me – at her age! I mean I'm boasting, but when I walked down the street shop windows just used to shatter! What a din!

Doctor I can quite well believe it. After all, you're still a beautiful woman . . .

Rosa I know!

Doctor It's the truth . . . Anyway, let's get back to your husband. Now, take a good look at his hands. Do you recognise them?

Rosa No, not now . . . They look like two pieces of boiled meat . . . But afterwards, yes, when he gets better . . . because he will get better, won't he Professor . . . promise me that he will get better . . .

Doctor Madam . . . we will do everything we can . . . Your husband is a very strong man . . .

Rosa Ah yes, he's strong, very strong! He had such energy, such good health! He would never hold back from anything. When the Unità festival[3] came round, for example . . .

Doctor So. You're communists are you?

Rosa Oh, we've been communists for generations, from father to son . . . it's a custom we hand down in our family . . . As I was saying, the Unità festival, he was always there, in charge of everything: he used to put up the stalls, sell the books, and buy them too . . . In his Party branch too, in the discussions, he would put forward all the arguments, and then put forward the counter-arguments, as well as the self-criticism. But don't go thinking that he was a fanatical bigot . . . No, far from it, he was always having arguments, particularly with the leadership . . . even if he had accepted the Third Road to socialism . . . he was also prepared for the Fourth Road ring road to socialism, and the by-pass of the Fifth Road . . . because, as Karl Marx says, 'the roads to socialism are infinite'! Of course, she was always there behind him . . . the bitch, egging him on! Because she's an extremist. She doesn't even have a Party card . . . Nothing! Not even a Socialist Party card! She's one of those intellectuals who are always trying to teach us, the working class, everything. The kind of people who are crazy about the masses, but can't stand crowds! She isn't here is she? She isn't hiding under the bed?

Inadvertently, ROSA *grabs hold of one of the strings and pulls on it. This results in the dummy leaping off the bed. Everyone, including the* DOCTOR *, rushes to rearrange it.*

Doctor No. Madam, what are you doing? Don't touch!

Rosa Oh my God! What have I done? Have I broken him? Hey, I'm not the only one to blame! Why do you leave the wires hanging down like that . . . Why don't you put up a notice: 'Don't pull on the wires!' Oh, what a fright . . . I can feel the tears coming on again . . . (*To an* ORDERLY) Excuse me, do you have a Kleenex so that I can blow my nose . . .

Orderly Here you are, madam . . .

Rosa Poor Antonio . . . And how's – he – going to blow his nose now that he hasn't got one?

During this exchange, the three ORDERLIES *lift the* SURGEON *up, into a horizontal position. From this curious position, he begins working on the dummy's face with swabs and forceps.*

Doctor Don't worry, madam, we'll make him another nose, and he'll be able to blow it whenever he wants.

Rosa Professor, do you always work in such an uncomfortable position? Another nose? Will you be transplanting one from a dead person? But supposing his body rejects it, and his nose comes off into his handkerchief while he's blowing it? No, no nose! I'd rather have him like this . . . streamlined.

Doctor No, no, no transplant! You are lucky, madam: our Institute is extremely advanced in plastic surgery operations.

The THREE ORDERLIES *now hold the* SURGEON *as high as they can. He spreads out his arms like an angel.*

Orderly Our Chief Surgeon is one of the best in the world!

Doctor It's true.

The PROFESSOR *is slowly returned to the ground.*

Rosa Professor, he's looking at me! Look, there with that corner of his eye peeking out from the swelling . . . He's seen me, he's recognised me . . .! I'm sure of it . . . Antonio, Antonio, it's me, your Rosa . . . As soon as I heard what happened, I forgot everything . . . Here I am, and I'm not bitter . . . In fact, to tell you the truth, Antonio, I'm actually happy that this terrible thing has happened . . . No, no, I don't mean that . . . What I mean is that I'm happy that I, your Rosa, can still be of use to you . . . I still love you, you know . . . I don't care if you used to go jogging with her, and eat brown rice and wheatgerm! . . . We'll forgive and forget, we'll get everything right, just as it was before . . . We'll bury the past.

The patient emits a groan.

No, Antonio, you misheard me. I didn't say that'd we'd bury – you –! Oh what a wally I am! But his jawbone here, it's all gone . . . there's just a big hole . . .

Doctor The mandible is indeed in very poor shape . . . We're going to have to replace it with a whole prosthetic apparatus . . .

Rosa Prosthetic? Whole apparatus?

Doctor Precisely! We rebuild it entirely, on the basis of the original bone structure: we remove the parts which are broken, and we replace them. Incidentally, you will have to supply me with some photographs. Do you have any recent ones?

At this point, enter from backstage the actor who plays the part of ANTONIO.

Antonio Excuse me . . . Excuse me . . . I'm going to have to interrupt at this point, because a misunderstanding is being created.

The ACTORS *on stage freeze.* ANTONIO *moves to the front of the stage and addresses the audience directly.*

The lights go down in the operating theatre. The ACTORS *exit.* ANTONIO *remains front-stage, and behind him, a platform is wheeled on. On it are two car seats and assorted scrap parts of motor cars. We are in a breaker's yard.*

Antonio In this play, I take the part of Antonio, Rosa's husband. But I am not the donor kebab that you see here on the operating table. That's someone else. So who is it? Well, in order to explain this, I'm going to have to put things in order, and go back 24 hours, to yesterday evening. So, last night, or rather at about two o'clock this morning, I, Antonio Berardi, Fiat worker, was parked in my car in a secluded spot on the outskirts of Turin. To be precise, on the road that runs along the canal bank by Barriera di Milano, you know. No, I was not alone. I was with a woman . . . and to be honest, it was not even the woman that I'm living with at the moment, Lucia, the one that Rosa calls the 'bitch' . . . Now, don't go getting the wrong idea . . . This wasn't some kind of erotic adventure . . . She was a colleague from work . . . a shop steward. We were discussing redundancies. She told me that the other day at Fiat, they sacked two workers for absenteeism – and then they discovered they'd been dead for a month! Well, one thing led to another and we made love, and afterwards I told Lucia about it . . . (*Calling offstage*) Lucia, could you come in please . . .

Enter LUCIA. *She goes and sits down..*

. . . at dawn this morning, when we met in a car-breaker's yard run by a friend of mine . . . She didn't exactly mince her words.

Lucia So this is what you mean by exploring closer relations between the union leadership and the rank and file!

Antonio Good God! You're a worse moraliser than my wife! You don't realise what a mess I'm in . . . It's a matter of life and death!

Lucia Life and death? I'm sorry, Antonio . . . Go ahead, tell me . . . I promise you, I won't say another word . . .

Antonio Thank God for that.

Lucia Except that . . .

Antonio Ah, Ah, Ah. Why did I get involved in all this? There I was, at peace with the world, with the shop steward . . . on the canal bank . . . having a cuddle . . . no mean feat in the back of a 128 . . . when all of a sudden I see two cars tearing along, neck and neck jostling for position. I said: 'Look at those stupid lunatics, racing around at this time of night, especially on this kind of ground. They're liable to skid!' I'd hardly finished speaking, when one of the cars skidded . . . A terrible crash! The Fiat 132 (I knew it was a 132 . . . It's the sort we make in our plant) . . . The 132 ended up in a mangled heap, not twenty yards away . . . Then the other one comes along, bounces off it, and ends up nose-down in the mud . . . I said, 'I expect they're both dead then'.

Lucia I can well believe it. So, what did you do?

Antonio What was I supposed to do? I jumped out of my 128, just as I was, to see if I could save anyone. The car doors were jammed. I kicked them. I got them open. A cloud of smoke poured out . . . My God, my eyes were streaming . . . I was coughing . . . but I carried on, all the same: I dragged them out . . . One, two, three . . . They were asphyxiated. All of them, asphyxiated. I tried to pull out the fourth one. You should have seen the state of him. He was all smashed up . . . He was sitting next to the driver's seat. He'd smashed his face against the windscreen. Squashed flat! Flat as a 100-lire piece! All he needed was the writing round the edge: Republic of Italy . . .

Lucia Yes. All right, all right, what the hell.

Antonio So, I dragged him out, dragged him out by the armpits. I was just laying him out on the grass, when suddenly Boom! The engine went up! Both of us were caught, full frontal, by the flames.

Lucia Oh, Christ!

Antonio Well, no, not both of us . . . only him, actually. Because, as soon as I saw the flames, instinctively I pulled up our squashed friend and put him in front of me. You know how it is, it's instinct . . . One doesn't think . . . A spur of the moment thing!

Lucia So.

Antonio So now he's all on fire, so I started pulling all his clothes off: his jacket, his shirt, and his trousers . . . But he still carried on burning, because he was covered in oil which had caught fire. So I took off my jacket and wrapped it round him . . . to put out the flames.

Lucia Well, I must say, you're a dirty old man, but you've got a big heart.

Antonio Yes, I've got a tiny brain and all! Because, if I'd minded my own business . . .

Lucia Speaking of your own business, what about your colleague, the shopfloor delegate . . . Did she delegate everything to you? Did she just sit there and watch?

Antonio No, she didn't. As soon as she saw the flames, she grabbed up her stuff, just as she was, half naked, and ran off down the road, in her high-heel shoes . . . tac-tac-tac . . . . flobber, flobber, flobber, stark naked.

Lucia So, she was half naked, eh? And you too?

Antonio No! I had my jacket on . . .! No trousers, but a jacket, yes . . . Do you mind! Let's have a bit of decency . . .!

Lucia Just a moment, Antonio, do you have any idea of who it was that you pulled out of the burning car?

Antonio No. Why, do you?

Lucia I've a suspicion. But hasn't it even occurred to you that it wasn't just an ordinary road accident, but that it might have been . . . I don't know . . . an attempted kidnap?

Antonio What do you take me for, an idiot? Obviously it occurred to me. But only afterwards! When they began shooting at me with guns!

Lucia Shooting at you? But who? When?

Antonio For heaven's sake, listen, will you let me tell the story as it happened . . .

Lucia But . . .

Antonio Oi! Don't keep interrupting!

Lucia I won't say another word.

Antonio So. I dragged squashy out of the car, he was all on fire. I wrapped him in my jacket. I noticed that the people whom I'd dragged out who I thought were all suffocated, were starting to cough; they were coming round. So, I shouted over to them: 'Oi! stop all that coughing, and come over here, help me take your friend, your colleague, to hospital, because he's dying here.' They completely ignored me. They were going round on all fours . . . Just like constipated sheep. What was I supposed to do? Wait for a vet? I picked up Features and took him over to my car, the 128. I put him inside. I pulled on my trousers. I started the engine, and at that moment: Bang! Bang! Who was that? It was our suffocated friends. They were coughing and shooting at the same time. Bastards! Good God, I'd saved their lives, and, by way of thanks, they start popping off at me?

Lucia What did you do?

Antonio I shone my headlights in their eyes, and tried to run them over . . . Whoosh! They leapt out of the way . . . like frogs. I swerved round the other car, and you'd have thought they were dead . . . But no: Bang, Bang! It was like Starsky and Hutch. Like Sam Peckinpah come back to life, and it wasn't in slow motion either. I was lucky to get away with my goolies.

Lucia Goodness, it's sending shivers down my spine . . . What kind of world are we living in?!

Antonio Yes, you said it! But it's not over yet . . . I drove into town, and got as far as Porta Susa, where there's a Red Cross ambulance parked by the roundabout.

Lucia That's right, that's where they park.

Antonio Exactly . . . And I called the stretcher bearers to come over. They turn up and start giving a bit of that: 'Dear, oh dear, oh dear, look at the state of this one. Who did this, then, eh? What is it – factory-fresh or home-made?' I saw right away that they thought that it was me who had done it. 'Look,' I said, 'Let's just get him down to the hospital, to casualty. There'll be a policeman there. I can explain everything to him.' 'OK.' They loaded Features into the ambulance . . . and told me to follow them in the car. As soon as we got to the first crossroads, whoosh, I scarpered!

Lucia But you're crazy! Why did you go and do a thing like that?

Antonio Because I was afraid. All of a sudden I imagined myself in the police station, with the police interrogating me. I mean, who was ever going to believe me. Who was ever going to believe that I was on the canal bank by accident, and that I was with a girl whose name I can't even remember . . . At the very least they would have arrested me, beaten the shit out of me . . .

Lucia You're right, it's enough to make anyone lose their head. More to the point, though, Antonio, do you know who it was you saved?

Antonio No, why? Do you?

Lucia Yes. It was Agnelli.

Antonio Agnelli? Don't talk rubbish: Agnelli!

Lucia I'm not talking rubbish. They said so this morning, on television. A news flash: 'The kidnapping took place at about two o'clock this morning in Barriera di Milano'. So he *must* be your squashed friend.

Antonio Agnelli?! I saved Agnelli? Me? I took him in my arms, I wrapped him in my jacket . . . Me! If my workmates get to hear about this at Mirafiori⁴, they'll line me up and run me over with tractors . . . with bulldozers! They'll bang me up against a wall and . . . splosh! splosh! splosh! . . . they'll gob me to death! . . . Just think, with all this bronchitis that's going around! But why didn't you tell me, instead of letting me ramble on like an idiot . . .

Lucia I wanted to be sure. I didn't interrupt you so as not to influence you. But what a mess! Do you realise the trouble that you've got yourself into? This'll teach you to go out whoring with female shop stewards!

Antonio Obviously, it's my just reward isn't it? 'Anyone who goes whoring with female shop stewards is punished by God, who makes him save Agnelli's life!' Get on with your story! What else did the telly have to say!?

Lucia Well, first of all they gave the news that Agnelli had been kidnapped, and then they said that, according to statements by some of his bodyguards, the kidnappers drove up alongside the car in which Agnelli was travelling, and fired a bazooka through the rear window.

Antonio A bazooka. They used a bazooka?! Of course they did! Nowadays they only use bazookas . . . it's safer . . . more convenient. 'Excuse me mate. Have you got a light?' Bang!

Lucia The window shattered, and the shell went off inside the car, giving off a cloud of poison gas which paralysed his bodyguards.

Antonio Ah, so that smoke was gas?! It's true, they were really coughing badly.

Lucia Then they said that when the bodyguards came to they woke up just in time to see one of the terrorists' accomplices, 'who had clearly been parked on the embankment for some time'.

Antonio Accomplice, eh? For some time! Like any self-respecting accomplice, I was parked on the embankment . . . Oi! Terrorists! I know I'm your accomplice, but do me a favour! Get a move on! I'm a bit parky because I've got no trousers on! So as to be less conspicuous.

Lucia Antonio, they said that Agnelli was unconscious, and that you loaded him into a red Fiat 128 and drove off.

Antonio So . . . I'm done for, now . . . I'm an accomplice! Or rather, the main organiser of the kidnap . . . What an idiot! You go and play the Good Samaritan, you go and save the life of bosses who gamble with your own life like they were playing gin rummy. The bastards!

Lucia Antonio, calm down. Agreed, they're bastards, but there's no point in getting all dramatic about it. You'll see. As soon as Agnelli regains consciousness in the hospital, he'll explain that he is Gianni Agnelli, and he'll tell how you saved his life, and everything will be fine and dandy.

Antonio Well that is very likely, isn't it! 'Hello. I am Gianni Agnelli . . . I demand to see immediately, the trouserless engineering worker who saved my life . . . Where is he, I feel I love him! I shall marry him . . . We'll be married . . . In white!' Leave it out . . . with the knocking that he took, it'll be a miracle if he even remembers his name when he wakes up . . . 'Who are you?' 'Ga, Ga, Ga, Ga!'

Lucia Is he really in such a state?

Antonio No – I'm – the one in the state! The ambulance men got a good full-frontal of me, from three yards away! My picture's going to be in all the papers today . . . My identikit! And underneath there'll be a caption: 'Head of the terrorist organisation in Lombardy, Piedmont, and Ticino!'

Lucia You're exaggerating, as usual. For a start, there's no identikit in the papers. (*She pulls a newspaper out of her handbag and gives it to* ANTONIO)

Antonio What newspaper is that?

Lucia A special edition. I bought it an hour ago.

Antonio Jesus – they're really quick! (*He reads*) '*Fury as Tearaway Terrorists Nab Fiat Supremo*. Fifty-three groups claim responsibility . . . *Barriera Bombing. It's the Mafia again*. President Reagan demands televised debate with Frank Sinatra . . . *Bishop of Durham Speaks Out*. See page ten . . . *Andreotti Lashes Bazooka Bandits*. Andreotti claimed that the state will not give into blackmail, and asked to be made managing director of two banks. He also asked for Life Senatorships for everybody involved in the P2 Freemason Scandal . . . *Pontiff Pips Premier*. His holiness the Pope pipped the Prime Minister to the post and offered himself as hostage in Agnelli's place; together with thirteen cardinals, ten of whom are black . . . *Play Terrorist Bingo and win a Panda.'*

Lucia There, you see? It's the usual mad house . . . But there's not a word about you, and about Agnelli in hospital. Listen, Antonio. Tomorrow you should go into work at Fiat, as if nothing had happened.

Antonio You're crazy . . . I'm going to go down there, and say, 'Here I am' . . . Here I am . . .!

Lucia Where?

Antonio Down here . . . (*He points to the newspaper*) *'Factory worker in Frazzle Mystery.* Forty-year-old Antonio Berardi, skilled worker at the Mirafiori, was admitted to hospital by persons unknown earlier this morning. His face was severly disfigured by burns. His wife, Rosa Berardi, has been traced thanks to documents which the victim had in his jacket.' . . . I left everything in my jacket! I left my driving licence, my Party card . . . my Union card . . . (*He stops short, and bursts out laughing*) Ha, ha, ha!

Lucia What's so funny?

Antonio Agnelli, a member of the union now! If he dies now, they'll give him a funeral with red flags! . . . 'Rosa Berardi has been invited to attend the hospital in order to identify her husband . . .'

Lucia Hey, Antonio, Rosa's bound to identify Agnelli as you.

Antonio Look, you're going to have to stop seeing my wife as some kind of mental defective. This is a trap, and I'm not falling for it.

Lucia What do you mean, a trap?

Antonio They've written that on purpose . . . so that I go to the hospital, like some prize twat: 'Hello, Rosa, look, don't identify me as me, because here I am, large as life, and this fellow is somebody else.' Bang! Immediate arrest of halfwit terrorist. Why don't *you* go and take a look.

Lucia You're right. I'll go to the hospital and see what's going on . . .

Antonio (*Now turns directly to the audience*) Now we can get back to the operating theatre, and pick up where we left off . . .

Re-enter the DOCTOR, ROSA *and the* WARD ORDERLIES. *Exit* ANTONIO *and* LUCIA.

Doctor Incidentally, madam, you will have to bring me some photographs. Do you have any recent ones?

Rosa No, Professor, I'm sorry, but since my husband left me, I haven't really been bothered with having photographs taken. I still work as a hairdresser in town . . . But I've let myself go a bit, you know.

Doctor But no, you misunderstand . . . Not photographs of you . . . photographs of your husband . . .

Rosa Ah, yes, how stupid of me. I do have some – very fine ones. Where's my handbag. (*She pulls out from her handbag two large photographs of* ANTONIO, *and hands them to the* DOCTOR) They're recent . . . I hope you don't mind if there's a little bit cut off but, you see, the bitch was with him in the photo, and I can't really be expected to carry the bitch round with me in my handbag all day . . . so I chopped her off and hung her on the wall . . . with two pins in her eyes, so as . . . people tell me that it really does work, you know . . . An Indian custom . . . Or maybe African . . . Doctor, you wouldn't happen to know if she's likely to . . . go blind? No. Will they do? Look what a nice face!

Doctor Yes, good, they are fairly clear . . . We are lucky. These will help us a lot in the projections.

Rosa Projections?

Doctor Yes. First you project the image of the patient's face, from the photograph, and then you reconstruct it around a wax skull.

Rosa A wax skull?

Doctor Exactly. First we reconstruct the bone structure, and then the whole thing is covered with skin.

Rosa With skin? With artificial skin? Like leatherette?

Doctor No, not artificial skin, real skin! His skin! We take it from here . . . from the buttocks . . .

Rosa From his bum? You're going to put bits of his bum on his face . . .?! Oh, Antonio, my poor Antonio, what a terrible situation . . .

ROSA *suddenly moves away from the patient and inadvertently leans on a lever. This releases the central operating theatre lamp, which crashes down onto the dummy. General pandemonium ensues.*

Doctor No! Not the lever!

A musical interlude follows. As the lamp falls, enter the POLICE INSPECTOR. *He approaches the* DOCTOR.

Inspector A moment . . . Allow me . . . Are these recent photographs?

Rosa Yes . . . Is he a surgeon?

Inspector No, I am the police inspector.

Rosa Ah, police? And are you here to find out who did this streamlining job on my husband?

Inspector I might be.

Rosa Well there's no point in asking him. Go and ask those bastards at Fiat. Go and ask Agnelli.

Inspector Now, madam, there's no need to bring Mr Agnelli into all this, particularly at a time like this. Who knows where the poor man is at this moment?

Rosa Antonio, I promise you that if they ever find him, I'll go looking for him, and I'll mash his face up just like yours!

Doctor Madam, is all this really necessary? I've already told you he doesn't understand . . .

Rosa Oh yes he does! There's a glint in his eye . . .

Enter an ORDERLY *with a sheet of paper in his hand. He goes over to the* DOCTOR.

Orderly Excuse me, Professor, there's somebody here. Says they're a relative of the patient, Antonio Berardi, and asks if it's possible to see him.

Rosa Let's have a look . . . Who is this relative?

Orderly I don't know. Here's the details.

Rosa Can I see them, eh . . .?

Doctor No, madam, please. I am the doctor here, until proven otherwise, and it's me who decides who is to be let in. Lucia Rismondi.

Rosa *It's the bitch!* She has the nerve to pass herself off as a relation, just because she was sleeping with my husband! The whore!

Doctor Madam, calm down.!

Rosa Calm down? Why should I calm down? I'm furious! Humiliating me like this! Here I am, heartbroken, with my husband looking like a Michelin Man . . . all wrapped up like a packet of fish fingers, and *she* comes here just to spite me.

Doctor Madam, will you stop that! I can't stand scenes! I warn you that if you don't start behaving very civilly indeed, I shall have you shown out of here, and I shall not let you come back to visit your husband for at least a month. Clear?

Rosa (*Looking at the* DOCTOR *in amazement*) Dont't you talk to me like that. Just who do you think you are talking to in that arrogant tone? Use it on some patient in a coma. Not on me. I'm involved in politics, me! I've opened birth control clinics. I'm not some timid woman who lets herself be put down by people who shout! No, sir! I am the patient's wife! I can come in when I want! That's the law! My husband, after all, is in a coma! And if you've got something to say about it I'll stage such a sit-in, right here and now.

Inspector Madam, listen, I am conducting investigations precisely in order to discover what has happened to your husband. It's possible that this woman might be able to give us some useful information.

Rosa But she doesn't know anything, because she never saw anything! Anyway, she's also about to go blind, with the pins! Isn't she, Doctor?

Doctor Get out! Get out!

Rosa (*She moves off, reluctantly, but after a few steps, she faints*) Oh, God, I feel ill . . . Oh, my head . . .

Doctor (*The* DOCTOR *lifts her up*) Madam, please don't start play-acting . . .

They help her to sit down.

Would you pass me the smelling salts. Come on . . . Come on . . . take a deep breath. (*He forces* ROSA *to smell the salts*)

Rosa Cough, cough! Cough . . . I'm suffocating . . . Professor, You're mad! What is this vile stuff you're making me breathe . . .? Cough . . . There, now I really do feel ill!

Doctor No, you're not ill . . . Come on, be good, get out of here . . .

Rosa Let me get my breath. (*She breathes, very ostentatiously*) I'd like to make a self-criticism.

Doctor Oh my god.

Rosa You're right. I've behaved really badly . . . I've been selfish. When all's said and done, that poor girl has the right to see my husband too. If she's fallen in love, it's hardly her fault . . . She's so young and pretty too . . . She's educated. She's got a degree! She's a doctor! She could have taken up with a professor like yourself, or, if the worst came to the worst, with an Inspector, like yourself . . . But no . . . She decided to choose my husband . . . a man old enough to be her father . . . I mean any wife should feel proud, don't you think? I am. I'm really happy . . . Please, Inspector, don't send me away. I would really like to meet her . . .

Inspector OK . . . OK. As long as you stay there and keep your mouth shut.

Doctor Alright, Inspector, shall we ask her in? (*He signals to the* ORDERLIES *to put a screen in front of the bed, so that* LUCIA *does not see the patient at once*)

Inspector All right. Get her in here!

Doctor Show her this way please.

Enter LUCIA. *There is a moment of embarrassment and tension.*

Lucia Mrs Berardi . . . Please excuse me if I . . . Perhaps I shouldn't have . . . I know . . .

Rosa Oh, you were right. I'm very pleased to meet you. I'm sure he will be pleased to see you as well, although I don't suppose he will recognise you! (*She embraces her formally*)

Lucia Hasn't he regained consciousness yet?

Rosa Yes he has . . . he definitely recognised me. Of course it might be more difficult with you, though, because he hasn't known you very long . . .

Lucia Are you sure that it really is him?

Inspector A moment, excuse me . . . Miss, please, would you please mind stepping over to the bed . . .

Rosa Wait a moment, Inspector.

Lucia Inspector?

Rosa Yes. He's here for the investigation. Don't let him rush you. Be brave . . . He's got nothing left . . . Only two ears . . .

Lucia (*going up to the bed, and barely glancing at the dummy*) Oh, my god, it's really horrible! It's him . . . It's him . . . (*She clings to* ROSA)

Doctor Are you sure? By what do you recognise him?

Rosa From his hands, no . . .?

Inspector Come along, don't lead her on!

Rosa Who's leading her on?

Lucia: By his ears.

Inspector: By his ears?

Lucia Yes, because I've studied those ears inch by inch . . .

Doctor You've studied his ears?

Rosa What an intellectual!

Lucia Yes, you see . . . I practise acupuncture . . . and I've even been to China on a training course . . . And since Antonio suffered from sinusitis . . .

Rosa Yes, yes, sinusitis . . . it's true . . . he had it really badly!

Lucia To cure him, I used to stick needles in his ears . . .

> ROSA *mimes sticking needles in her ears and at the same time starts running on the spot.*

> That's how I recognise him. As you may know, Professor, every ear has its own particular physiognomy . . . In fact, if you take a wax mould of the auditory pavilion, you get a shape which looks like a little foetus, which is none other than a miniature portrait of how we were in our mother's wombs.

Inspector Like seeing a snapshot of yourself as a baby!

Rosa A foetus in your ear!! I'll have to tell them that at the clinic!

Doctor It's true! Our police forensic departments no longer use the usual fingerprint system, but take wax moulds of the auditory chambers of their suspects!

Inspector You mean every time you're arrested, wallop, a dollop of hot wax in your earhole! Incredible! You scientists are amazing! Well, that wraps it up: it's him, Antonio Berardi. Doctor, I would like to thank you for your co-operation.

Lucia and Rosa Don't mention it . . .

Inspector Let's go and have a drink.

Rosa Well, Antonio, you've been positively identified as my very own Antonio Berardi. She's a bit of a know-it-all, isn't she Antonio . . . *Doctor, Doctor*, he's trying to say something . . .

> ROSA *suddenly turns away from the patient. Somehow she contrives to lose her balance. She supports herself by grabbing one of the wires hanging down. The dummy flies up in the air, amid scenes of general pandemonium.*

BLACKOUT

MUSICAL INTERLUDE

ACT 1

Scene 2

When the lights come up again, we find ourselves in the same scene as before.

The bed with the dummy on it has disappeared. On stage are ROSA *and the* DOCTOR.

Doctor Madam, this may seem a bit presumptuous, but you're going to have to give us credit for the miraculous things that we've managed to achieve. You will see . . . a masterpiece!

The DOUBLE *is wheeled on stage in a wheelchair pushed by three* WARD ORDERLIES. *His face is swathed in bandages. Everyone bustles around him, busily removing the bandages, to reveal his face.*

The DOUBLE'*s face is encased in a kind of mask of elastic tapes. Small rings are fixed to various positions of the tapes – one on his chin, one on his nose, one on each cheek, and one on his forehead. Wires or cords are connected to each ring, and they pass through pulleys in an overhead metal or wooden frame. The other ends come down to stage level. Each* ORDERLY *holds one or two of these wires.*

As the action unfolds, ROSA *says:*

Rosa Oh, the suspense is killing me! It reminds me of a film I saw when I was a girl: 'The Living Mummy!' where they unbandaged someone just like this . . . There he is . . . Look . . . It's him . . . It's him . . .! Frankenstein!

Doctor But what are you saying, madam, he's perfect!

Rosa Oooh. Well done . . . You've caught him really well . . . Mind you all those stitches all over his face.

Doctor Yes, but they can't be helped . . . In a few days they will disappear, though, some of them will dissolve . . . and with the others, you just pull one end, and out they come.

Rosa But if you pull on one end of the thread, won't he come undone, and won't his face fall all over the floor?

Doctor Nein nein.

Rosa I'm sorry. You can tell, I'm so happy I'm beginning to talk rubbish again. Oh, Antonio, if you could only see yourself . . . You're almost better than before! Antonio, how do you feel? Tell me!

The man doesn't move.

Doctor Gently, madam, gently . . . He has to get used to speaking again . . . We must proceed gradually . . . You should remember that we have rebuilt his entire jawbone and palate.

Rosa Ah yes, I suppose now he's just running in.

Doctor So leave it to me. Mr Berardi, try opening your mouth slowly, let's see if you can do it . . .

The DOUBLE *does as he says*

Well done . . .

The DOUBLE's *attempts to speak are assisted by the* WARD ORDERLIES, *and by the* DOCTOR. *They pull on the various wires, and through mime amplify his facial movements. This gives the impression that every movement of his mouth is brought about by operating the 'machine'.*

Rosa It's opening, it's opening!

Doctor And now, try with me, repeat after me: Ahaaa . . .

Double Ahaaa . . .

The DOCTOR *and the* ORDERLIES *continue their mime action.*

Rosa He said Ahaaa!

Doctor Please keep quiet, madam. Once again: Ahaaa . . . Oooh . . .

Rosa Come on, Antonio, say Oooh, as the doctor tells you!

Double Oooh . . .

Doctor No, no, first Ahaaa, then Oooh! Pay attention to me, not to your wife! Once again: Ahaaa . . . Oooh . . .

Double Ahaaa . . . Oooh . . . Eheee . . .

Rosa He said 'E' . . . all by himself! How intelligent!

Doctor No, not at all! He mustn't do that! Mr Berardi, you must make only the sounds that I ask you to make!

Rosa Alright, but if he decides he wants to go 'Eheee', don't you think that it's a bit much to stop him?

Doctor Madam, you should realise that the sound 'Eheee' requires the jawbone to extend to its maximum limit, with the risk that it might come out of its mastoid socket.

Rosa So does that mean that my Antonio, when he talks will never be able to say 'e's'? Here, so you won't be able to say wheatgerm, then, will you?

Doctor No, no, he – will – be able to say 'e's' too, but later! First he must make the intermediate sounds, like: Braaa, Brooo, Bray.

Double Braaa . . . Brooo . . . Bray . . . (*repeated several times, evolving in Satchmo impersonation*)

Doctor There, that's just perfect! And now, say: gastric . . . gastropod . . .

Double Gaaastric, gaasopo . . .

Doctor No, articulate it properly: Gas; tero-pod . . .

Double Troppo . . . Gastopo . . . Braaa, Brooo, Bray!

Doctor Silence! And now say: astronaut, concupiscence, manumission.

Rosa But Professor, have you gone mad? What are these words that you're making him say? He's never going to say words like that . . . He's a worker . . . Make him say the words that he's going to use every day: wage packet, lay-offs, redundancies . . . Astronaut? Why, we don't even know one!

Doctor Listen, I'm the one who knows how to teach! Come along, Mr Berardi: astronaut, manumission, concupiscence.

Double Conc . . . Concup . . . Concup . . . Piss off!

Doctor What???!

Rosa See, now you've upset him!

The DOUBLE *gets up and goes to walk out towards the exit.*

ROSA *tries to stop him.*

Rosa I'll stop him. I'm his wife. Antonio, you can't go out . . .

She approaches her husband, who is walking like Frankenstein. She tries to stop him.

Antonio, stop! But look how he's walking! You must have made a mistake somewhere! Antonio, you're not a robot!

Double Don't – you – start too, madam!

Rosa Professor, did you hear? He called me madam. He's pretending he doesn't recognise me. But Antonio, dear, I'm Rosa, I'm your wife!

Double What do you mean, wife . . . wife, indeed? F . . . F . . . F . . . Forget it!

He goes out, dragging the wires behind him. The WARD ORDERLIES *follow him, trying to untangle the wires.*

Rosa Did you hear that?! Where's he going, Professor? Stop him!

Doctor No, let him move about a bit, let him take a little walk. Anyway, where's he going to go? He'll go to his room. And you, madam, don't go feeling all hurt. You must understand, after all these months of tension, with one operation after another . . . it's natural that he's on edge. Instead, you should think about the happy outcome of this whole experiment . . . treatment.

Rosa What happy outcome? I've been visiting him for months and months, and he's never even looked at me. Then, finally, he speaks! And all that comes out is Braaa, Brooo, Bray . . . and then he says: 'What do you mean, wife . . .?!'

Enter the POLICE INSPECTOR.

Inspector Excuse me, Professor, did you give the prisoner . . . sorry, the patient, permission to leave?

Doctor Ja, just to go back to his room.

Inspector But he's not going back to his room. He's taken the lift down to the ground floor, to the way out.

Doctor My God. Stop that man.

Inspector Already done. I've despatched two officers to persuade him to rejoin us. Only our vigilance prevented him from doing a runner.

Rosa Doing a runner? Have you seen him walk?

Inspector Exactly . . . Listen, madam, would you mind stepping outside for a moment? I have something private to say to the Professor.

Rosa Yes, yes, I'm going. People are always throwing me out. I'll go and find Antonio . . . I'll give him a bit of my speech therapy . . . I'll teach him to say: I love you Rosa . . . I'm leaving the bitch . . . I'm coming back to you . . .' You can stick your astronaut up your manumission. (*With these words,* ROSA *exits*)

Inspector So, Professor, everything's sweet?

Doctor Yes. We're progressing well. We're building up a basic vocabulary for him. In a couple of days he will be speaking almost as well as you.

Inspector Magic. I'd like to start straight away putting a few simple questions to him . . .?

Doctor Yes, but only under my control.

Inspector Yes, yes, you can stay . . . In fact, you can give us a hand. Would you mind if I invite the Examining Magistrate in . . .? (*Without waiting for an answer he calls offstage*) Your Honour, step this way.

Enter the EXAMINING MAGISTRATE

Professor . . . No, you can make your own introductions. I'm very bad at names.

Enter a POLICEMAN *with a portable typewriter.*

This is my assistant . . . You know, to take down his statement.

Doctor What statement? Leaving aside the fact that I still don't know what you suspect him of . . .

Examining Magistrate Well, for a start, we have discovered that the red Fiat 128 registered in Berardi's name is the same car that the terrorists . . .

The INSPECTOR, *standing behind the* DOCTOR, *signals abruptly to the* EXAMINING MAGISTRATE *to keep quiet.*

Now then, what were you saying about the patient?

Doctor But you surely can't think that the patient is ready . . . We must proceed gradually. It will be very difficult to get him to answer questions logically. Almost certainly, the trauma which caused his coma has flattened all his mnemonic-responsive anafracts.

Inspector Mnemonic-responsive anafracts? What does that mean?

The DOCTOR *goes and stands behind the* POLICEMAN, *who is sitting on a wheeled office chair, and has put his typewriter on one of the pieces of theatre equipment (an encephalogram recorder) which is also on wheels. The* DOCTOR, *carried away with his explanation, grasps the* POLICE-MAN's *head, and describes what's in it. Then he pushes the wheeled* POLICEMAN, *together with his typewriter, to centre-stage.*

Doctor You see, in the central-posterior part of the brain, known as the mnemechaea, there is a space which we might call the memory warehouse. In this warehouse there are thousands of relays, which, when activated, switch on a number of tapes, on which are stored memories, words, sensations, in short, everything that has happened in our lives . . .

Inspector So, the trauma will have wiped all his tapes?

The INSPECTOR *too manhandles the junior* POLICEMAN's *head.*

Doctor No, not all of them, but most of them . . . It may be that, only one tiny, maybe insignificant detail will pop up. Everything else will have been erased.

Inspector What about if he just makes out that he can't remember, in order to avoid telling the truth?

The DOCTOR *and the* INSPECTOR *in turn grapple with the* POLICEMAN's *head, gesticulating. By now the* POLICEMAN *is thoroughly terrified.*

Doctor No, impossible! In this first phase – which we call the phase of innocence – the patient is not capable of practicing deception . . . because the fiction mechanism, which is the most exposed and ephemeral part of the brain, is always the first to be destroyed by any violent trauma.

Examining Magistrate In short,

The EXAMINING MAGISTRATE *also tries to get his hands on the* POLICEMAN's *head, but the* POLICEMAN *ducks out of the way to prevent him.*

they are no longer capable of pretending or lying. And does this happen in every case?

Doctor. Yes. Every case, but not in the case of politicians . . . For them, traumas have no effect.

Inspector Here he is . . . Hand built by robots

Enter the DOUBLE, *walking like a wobbly flamingo. They sit him down (centre-stage) on the wheeled office chair. When the* DOUBLE *enters, the* POLICEMAN *on wheels moves, together with his equipment, to the* DOUBLE's *left-hand side.*

Doctor Here you are, Mr Berardi, sit down here and relax . . . These gentlemen would like to ask you a few questions . . . Please, you mustn't force him. Let him free-wheel . . .

The DOUBLE *jerks his head, like a suspicious flamingo. He fixes on the* POLICEMAN, *eyeing him mischievously. The gag is repeated ad libitum.*

Inspector Of course. Freewheel . . . Tell us, where were you going to in such a hurry?

Doctor Try and answer, there's a good chap.

Double Gasteronomical . . . gastero . . . Could you repeat the question, please . . .

Inspector Where were you running off to?

Double Ruuuunning oooff . . . but I didn't want to run off . . . I ooonly waaanted to gooo . . .

Examining Magistrate Go where?

Double To Head Quarters . . .

Inspector What Head Quarters?

Double To the Heead Quaarters . . . which . . . after . . . over . . . theere! (*With a series of gestures, he describes stairs, lifts, doorbells, automatically opening doors*) Fruuut . . . tracht . . . Driing . . . Whoosh . . . Ching!

Doctor No, don't strain yourself, calm down, relax . . .

Examining Magistrate Yes, yes, relax, calm down. We only want to have a little chat . . . among friends . . .

Inspector And so as to help you . . . so that you can practice speaking.

Double Speeaking, among frieeends . . .? Are these your frieeends, Professor? (*He fixes a beady eye on the* POLICEMAN *like a pointer eyeing its prey*) What's he writing?

Inspector He's taking notes of what you say . . . so that we can monitor your progress.

Double Ah, yes? And theeen you'll leet me reead whaaat I said . . . and what he has written?

Inspector Certainly, and sign it . . .

Double Sign? Why sign?

Inspector No reason.

Double No, you're lying. Liar!

Inspector Cut that out.

Double Liar!!

Inspector Let's start from what you remember . . . For example, what's your name?

Double Well, everyone calls me Antonio . . . even the Professor . . . and that horrible woman . . . who's driving me mad . . . Antoniooo, Antonioooo . . . Antoniooooo . . . !

Examining Magistrate Your wife?

Double My wife? Yes, she says she is my wife but I don't remember her . . . becaause . . . Whoosh . . . Clang . . . Vroom . . . (*He starts waving his arms in vague and meaningless gestures*) Toniinoooo . . . Bruuuuu! Antoninoooo! Antonino-o-o-o . . .

Doctor Now then, now then, calm down, we won't talk about your wife any more . . .

Examining Magistrate We won't talk about your wife any more.

Inspector We won't talk about her any more.

Double We won't talk about my wife any more? Promise?

Inspector What do you mean, promise?

Double Promise!

Examining Magistrate and Doctor Promise!

Inspector Promise.

Double Dib, dib, dib.

Inspector: Look . . . Now . . . What about the accident?

Double (*Explodes like a madman, terrorised*) Ahaaa . . . Vrooom . . . Chugga-chugga . . . Bang . . . Kerrash . . . Biff . . . Oooooh.

Doctor No, look, you're doing this all wrong. You have to deal more tactfully, give him more leeway . . .

Examining Magistrate You're right. Listen, Mr Berardi, do you remember any particular details of your childhood?

Double My childhood! Yes . . . When I was a child . . . I liked motor cars, when I was a child . . .

Examining Magistrate But all little boys like motor cars . . .

Double But I liked them mooore! I lived in a greeeat big maaansion . . .

Doctor In childhood memories, everything is always big.

Double Yes. And when you're big it can be fucking enormous if you play your cards right. I remember when I was fourteen I was given a cowboy outfit.

Examining Magistrate Cowboy outfit?

Double Yes, and I've been running it ever since. Does that mean anything to you?

Policeman (*With typewriter*) . . . Cowboy outfit.

Inspector Scrub that out. Cowboy outfits.

Examining Magistrate What do you recall about your mother and your father?

Double My mother . . . I don't remember . . . No . . . Nothing . . . Mummy, no . . . At this moment, have no recollection of mother . . .

Examining Magistrate You don't remember?

Double I'm trying to remember . . . my mummy . . .

Inspector But don't strain yourself . . .

Double Wait a minute, I want to remember . . .

Examining Magistrate But you don't have to . . .

Double I want to remember! I loved my mummy. I don't remember my mummy. . . I haven't got a mummy! (*He cries, heartbroken*) I've looked everywhere in my memory, but I haven't got a mummy! (*He rests his head on the* INSPECTOR*'s shoulder*)

Inspector What are you doing?

Double Won't you give me a little cuddly-wuddly . . .

Inspector Cuddly-wuddly!

Double Just a little one . . .

Inspector Please, pull yourself together!

Double Please. Peezy, weezy, weezy.

Inspector Get off me. Stuff your mummy.

Double He said he wants to stuff my mummy! You'd better start praying that my memory doesn't come back, because if my memory does come back and I remember who I am and who I was . . . then . . . Whiiish, roar, roar! (*He becomes like King Kong*) I do remember my father, though . . . He always used to take me to see the cars . . .

Inspector Did he work at Fiat too?

Double Eh? Work? (*He slyly rests his head on the* INSPECTOR'*s shoulder*)

Inspector Pull yourself together . . .!

Double Oh look – I can laugh! Ah, it does me good to talk. I feel as if I'm getting better already.

Examining Magistrate Well done, carry on.

Double Gasteropod, astronaut . . . concupiscent . . . astronaut . . .

Policeman How do you spell gasteropod?

> *The* POLICEMAN *types frantically.*

Inspector But what are you typing there?

> *The* POLICEMAN *breaks off momentarily, and then starts again.*

Examining Magistrate Listen, would you feel up to telling us about the accident? Without straining yourself, though.

Double Ah . . . vrrr . . . beeee . . . ooonly little bits . . . I remember . . .! I was in a car . . . and there was another car . . . two cars . . .

Inspector There were two cars . . .

Double There was a race . . .

Examining Magistrate A chase . . . And you . . .

Double I was in the car . . .

Examining Magistrate Behind.

Double Behind . . .

Examining Magistrate and Inspector The car behind. Well done!

Double No, no . . . That's wrong . . .

Inspector What do you mean, no?

Double I made a mistake!

Inspector The first answer is always the one that counts!

Double Liar . . .

Inspector Don't let's start all that again!

Double Liar, liar . . . etc.

Doctor Now look, you really shouldn't put words in his mouth . . . (*He grabs the wheeled chair and pushes it upstage*) I told you! Let him free-wheel . . .

Inspector Very well, we'll let him free-wheel . . . (*He grabs the chair and hurtles it towards the audience*)

Double Yes . . . We're going . . . going fast . . . faster and faster . . . Bing, bang, bong . . . Crash . . . Smack . . . then . . . I can't remember . . . any more . . .

Inspector Try. There was a crash, a smash. What then. Blood, mangled bodies, headless torsos, smoke . . .

Double Ah, yes . . . flames . . . I'm on fire . . . HEEELP!

Inspector What's the matter with you, calm down!

Doctor I told you not to push him too far!

> *The* DOUBLE'S *jaw becomes dislocated.*

Doctor Oh I see what's happened here. Let go. Let go.

Double Thank you very much.

Doctor You're most welcome.

Inspector Not a lot to go on there Your Honour?

Examining Magistrate Indeed. We're going to have to try something else.

Double Then I remember a voice shouting out: 'Agnelli . . . They're carrying away Agnelli!'

Inspector Brilliant! Write that down!

Double Why brilliant? What does that mean? Would you care to explain to me who this Lawyer might be . . .? Because every now and then I have Agnelli on my mind . . .

Examining Magistrate I should think so too!

Double What?

Inspector Never mind. Now, what does the name Fiat mean to you . . .?

Double Fiat? Well, it's something almost . . . how can I say: like family . . . Fiat.

Examining Magistrate Your family?

Double Like something that belongs to me.

Doctor It's incredible how attached these Fiat workers are to their company!

Examining Magistrate And now, could you tell us a bit about your work . . .

Double Work?

Examining Magistrate What work did you do at Fiat?

Double Work?

Inspector Yes, work.

Double At Fiat . . .? Work?

Examining Magistrate Work . . .

Inspector Work

Examining Magistrate Working . . . Labouring . . .

Double Labouring . . . Work . . . Labour . . .

Examining Magistrate At Fiat . . .

Double Work . . . Labour?

Inspector Yes!

Double These words have no meaning for me . . .

Examining Magistrate (*The* EXAMINING MAGISTRATE *dictates to the* POLICEMAN *with the typewriter*) Filthy little skiver.

Inspector And what about profit, production? Do they mean anything to you?

Double Oh yes . . . A lot . . . And restructing . . . net profit . . . holding company . . . mobility of labour . . . summary sackings! Ha Ha!

Inspector And the word terrorism . . .? What does that mean to you?

Double It means: radical and accelerated development of the armed struggle with consequences which may be positive or negative depending on the general situation of conflictuality between the various combined interests.

Inspector Magic!

Doctor Magic!

Examining Magistrate Magic!

The EXAMINING MAGISTRATE *and the* INSPECTOR *are pleased. They laugh.*

Double Have I said the right thing?

Inspector Exactly the right thing!

Double I don't understand what I've said. I would like to know what is it that I've said.

Inspector Let's proceed. Let's see if you remember any contacts, for example, with foreign groups . . .

Double Yes, indeed . . . foreign groups . . . I remember . . .

Inspector Russians?

Double Russians . . . Oh yes . . . Russians . . . Many contacts . . .

Examining Magistrate Very good . . .

Double Magic. Was it magic? Are you pleased?

Examining Magistrate Yes, very pleased. And with Libyans?

Double Libyans? Libya . . . Ah yes . . . I remember . . . I paid a special visit to Libya. Armed men in uniform coming to meet me.

Examining Magistrate And did you talk about clandestine activities?

Double Yes: very clandestine! Traffic . . .

Examining Magistrate Traffic? Traffic of arms?

Double Yes, arms too . . . all kinds of arms . . . heavy and light . . .

Inspector Were you aware of why and for what purpose those arms were to be used?

Double Water.

Inspector What?

Double Mineral water, not carbonated!

Examining Magistrate What's he saying?

Doctor It's simple. He's saying he's thirsty . . .

Inspector Wait a moment, answer my question.

Double No, I'm thirsty . . . non-carbonated mineral water, cool but not iced!

Doctor Wait a minute, I'll see to it. I've got a fridge here.

Examining Magistrate Alright . . . get him his bloody water . . .

Double I hope it's not carbonated, because if I burp I'll blow the nose off!

Inspector I'll have a glass of that as well . . .

Double Oh, the funnel . . . Doctor, do you have the funnel?

Doctor Yes . . . yes . . . (*He pulls a funnel out of the fridge, and hands it to the* DOUBLE).

Examining Magistrate A funnel? What's that for?

Double In order to drink . . . Otherwise I spill it all over the place . . . (*He takes the funnel and sticks it into his neck, on the right hand side*) Doctor, could you help me to screw the funnel in? Ah, no, thanks, look, I've done it myself . . .

The DOCTOR *pretends to pour water into a glass.*

Your health! Gentlemen. (*He pours the water contained in the glass into the funnel*) . . . Brrr . . . It's cold.

Inspector Excuse me, where exactly have you poured it?

Double Ah, directly into my oesophagus . . .

Doctor Yes, for a few more months yet he won't be able to swallow either food or liquids by mouth.

Examining Magistrate So his food has to go through the funnel too?

Doctor Yes, only food that has been mashed and puréed . . . Everything by neck.

Double They purée everything for me, my starter, main course, dessert and coffee. No . . . not the coffee. I have special suppositories for the coffee.

Inspector Listen, would you mind if we get back to our little chat?

Double Yes, let's begin again . . . You were asking me if . . . I remember traffic of arms . . . and who were they aimed for. Vaguely . . . I remember the words: Wing, plot, right.

Examining Magistrate and Inspector Wing, plot, right?

Double Wing.

Examining Magistrate Plot.

Inspector Right.

Examining Magistrate Wing.

Double Plot. Right Wing Plot. That's right. And the word . . . 'destabilise' . . . But I didn't agree . . . but there was somebody . . . police, I think . . .

Examining Magistrate Police? Which police?

Double Well, I don't remember. Maybe ours . . .

Examining Magistrate Italian police? Special Branch? Secret services?

Double Very secret . . . Special services . . . One time they were on the point of exposing them . . . I knew about it . . . I was scared they'd implicate me too . . . Ah, now I remember the trial . . . Generals, ministers . . . then everything was exposed . . . and then covered up again! Whitewash.

Inspector Whitewash?

Policeman Generals . . . ministers . . . I didn't quite catch that. What he said before 'whitewash' . . .?

Inspector Don't write that down you pillock. Rub it out. Rub it all out!

Examining Magistrate No, not everything. Only from 'police' onwards . . .

Double Ah, now, that period I remember really well, really clearly . . . All the big-nobs, all their names . . . There was even an admiral involved . . . a judge . . . a minister . . .

Examining Magistrate Will you stop remembering.

Inspector Do something.

Double If I make a little effort, it'll all come back to me. I could name all five hundred of them . . . Now, I'll start in alphabetical order, from 'A' . . . The first is Andreot.[5] . . . the first is . . .

As the DOUBLE *is speaking the* EXAMINING MAGISTRATE *and the* INSPECTOR *try to interrupt him. He carries on regardless. The* INSPECTOR *signals to the* DOCTOR, *who immediately gives the* DOUBLE *an injection in the arm.*

... Andreot ... Andreottolo ... (*He loses his powers of speech, and breaks down*) Oh ... oh ... oh ...

Doctor There you are, Inspector. For ten minutes now he won't be able to either speak or hear.

Inspector Thank God for that. I don't think we need to hear any more, he's a terrorist ... Damned himself out of his own mouth ... Can't tell a lie.

Examining Magistrate In fact, it's almost criminal to take advantage of his honesty.

Inspector Your honour, don't forget that these are people who shoot you in the back!

Examining Magistrate Correct. We must never forget it! As we suspected, he was part of the gang who kidnapped Agnelli. He was done over in the rumble. Thinking he was about to snuff it, his colleagues got shot of him, bringing him here.

Inspector We're going to have to put the word about that he's turned into a poor babbling idiot, because if they suspect that we're getting him to talk, the terrorists in his group are liable to come here and do him in. Or the fellows from the secret services ...

Double I remember that ...

Examining Magistrate and Inspector Shut! Up!

The DOCTOR *rushes up and gives another injection.*

Double Ah ... oh ... never mind! (*He goes all floppy again*)

Inspector Right!

Examining Magistrate It couldn't be better if we'd arrested him red-handed ... Let's whisk him away without letting anybody know, and lock him in a total isolation cell, or even better, in a container like the anti-Terrorist squad do with theirs.

Inspector Yes, the anti-Terrorist squad!

Doctor Yes, go ahead. That'll just finish him off! He will become completely deranged, just like the Prime Minister.

Double (*coming round, mischievously*) Now I'll tell you all the names ... that I've remembered ...

Inspector and Examining Magistrate That's enough!

The action is repeated. The DOCTOR *gives him another injection. And again the* DOUBLE *goes all floppy.*

Double What a hit!

Doctor Listen to me – if you want him to carry on talking, leave him alone for a while. Don't show your faces for at least ten days.

Inspector But you must be joking, ten days? We can't ... We're holding the key to picking up a whole gang of terrorists, finding Agnelli – maybe even alive – and you ...

Doctor Alright, I understand ... Let's make it five days ...

Examining Magistrate No, no, two, three at most ...

Doctor Alright, as you think best . . . But then if his brain blows out, the responsibility will be yours, alright!?

Inspector Two days, and then we'll be back to interrogate him. We'll keep ten of our men here in the hospital, disguised as nurses and doctors . . .

Examining Magistrate Yes. Just so as to keep an eye on him and protect him.

Doctor Ten? Don't you think that's a bit many?

Examining Magistrate No, this is the best breakthrough that we've had to date. This fellow really is a Grade A Supergrass!

Inspector He talks so much that it's a pleasure to listen to him. He's worth more than Peci, Sandolo, Fioroni and Barbone[6] put together . . . He's a repentant terrorist and doesn't realise it!

Double (*Leaps to his feet like an uncoiled spring, and heads directly for the* EXAMINING MAGISTRATE *and the* INSPECTOR Now I remember the name of that Minister . . .

Examining Magistrate and Inspector Shut! Up!!

Double (*He pretends to go away, but suddenly turns round again*) I'll tell you . . .

Examining Magistrate and Inspector Shut! Up!

Double You shut up!

BLACKOUT

MUSICAL INTERLUDE

END OF ACT ONE

ACT II

Scene 1

We are in a big room in ROSA*'s house. There is a door in each of the three walls: the right-hand door gives onto the hallway landing. The centre door leads into the bedroom, and the left-hand door leads to the kitchen.*

Set: There's a table in the middle of the room. On it stands a plastic head with a wig on it. To the left stands a sideboard. Upstage left there is a television set. Upstage right, next to a chest of drawers, stands a free-standing coat-rack.

Up against the wall on the right stands a heavy wooden armchair, with arms and castors.

Front-stage, leaning up against the right-hand wall, is a small trolley. On it stands a papier mâché bust representing a two-headed mythical Greco-Roman character. There is also a standard lamp, from which hangs a clarinet.

As the lights come up, ROSA *and* LUCIA *enter from outside.* ROSA *has a shopping-bag, with her shopping. Front-stage centre we see a window. As* ROSA *says her first lines, she goes and flings the window open. Then, as she moves off to continue her dialogue with* LUCIA, *the window moves across the front of the stage and disappears into the wings Stage Right.*

Rosa Oh, Lucia, I *am* sorry. How long have you been waiting here for me?
Lucia Oh, about half an hour . . .
Rosa Oh, good heavens . . . If I'd known, I'd have hurried up. Excuse the mess . . . I was combing a customer's wig.

ROSA *shifts the wig, and puts it on the chest of drawers at the back of the stage.*

Lucia Oh, don't worry . . . In fact, I'm the one who should apologise for turning up just like this. The fact is, I was very worried. I don't know what's going on with Antonio. The hospital, won't let me in. They say that he's in a terribly volatile psychological state, with one crisis after another . . .
Rosa It's true, unfortunately . . .

ROSA *goes over the the window and flings it open.*

A breath of fresh air! They only let me in to see him for five minutes, and no sooner had I gone up to him than he started shouting: 'Go away! I don't want that pest of a woman anywhere near me! Go away! Go away!'

The window exits, stage right.

Lucia How dreadful! But what are the doctors saying? Are they doing anything for him?'

Rosa Well, they're doing what they can. They had the idea of driving Antonio out to the Fiat-Mirafiori plant and taking him to his old work section to try and budge something in his memory. When he went into the factory, he seemed quite at home. He was going round the various sections, cool as a cucumber, almost as if he owned the place. But when they put him in front of the assembly line, and stuck a welding gun into his hand, and told him: 'Come on, Antonio, weld . . . You've been doing it for so many years . . .' it was as if his brain exploded: his eyes bulging in his head, he began shouting like a madman: 'No! I'm not doing shitty work like this!'

LUCIA *barely succeeds in holding back a stifled laugh.*

'Take me away from this infernal machinery!'

Lucia (*Trying not to burst out laughing*) Ha, ha . . . ha, ha . . .

Rosa I mean it's not funny is it. What's the matter with you? Why are you laughing?

Lucia Excuse me . . . It's just a nervous reaction . . . To think of a man like Agnelli, I mean Antonio . . . reduced . . .

Rosa Ah yes, it's enough to drive you mad! Ah yes, I forgot to tell you. Last Thursday they brought him home for a couple of hours.

Lucia? Thursday? So you've seen him quite recently?

Rosa No, I was not there. They asked me to go out, because if Antonio sees me, he has another attack. Just imagine it. They bring my husband home, and I have to go out, as if I had scabies!

Lucia And did you manage to find out how he reacted here?

Rosa Yes. Indifferent. They told me that he went round the house, but didn't remember a thing . . . He didn't even remember his little statue over there, with the two faces, of Plutarch and Suetonius[7] . . .

She goes over to the papier mâché bust, which has a movable head. She takes it and turns it, revealing the second face.

. . . He was crazy about it! When he married me, he brought it as his dowry.

Lucia Ah, yes . . . he told me about it . . . he really had a thing about ancient history.

Rosa Precisely . . . And he didn't even glance at his books . . . And there was I, keeping them all properly for him, all in order . . . I said to myself, one of these days he's going to be coming back . . . He's going to get tired of the Bitch . . . I mean, of Lucia . . . Well, you know, these things can happen . . . a man leaves his wife, takes up with another woman, then he gets tired of the other woman, and goes back to his wife . . . That's life. I even saw it once, in a film. A very good film! Ooh . . . it *was* a good film! I saw it seven times! Afterwards, she, the girlfriend, became seriously ill, and died in excruciating pain . . .

LUCIA *looks at her.*

Come on, I'm only joking . . . It's true, she did die a horrible death . . . But I'm joking, Lucia, I like you . . . You've helped me through this tragedy, you've given me a hand . . . Of course, at first I had it in for you . . . In fact I put curses on you . . . Incidentally, how's your eyesight, Lucia?

Lucia Excellent!

Rosa Ah, I'm glad! So it was rubbish what they told me . . . Just as well it was lies . . . because otherwise, by now you'd be going round with a guide dog . . . and a white stick . . . Oh Lucia, what terrible times these are . . . Antonio has erased everything . . . Suetonius, the furniture . . . the table . . . me!

Lucia Cheer up, Rosa, you'll see . . . Antonio will get better . . .

Rosa No, Antonio won't get better . . . he'll never get better . . . I'm going to hang myself . . . Would you like a coffee?

Lucia Thank you, but only if you're making one for yourself . . .

Rosa Yes, it's alright. I'll make a coffee. I'll hang myself another day. (*Looking in her shopping-bag*) Where's the coffee? It's gone! I might have known it . . . I've only just bought it . . . and I forgot it at the greengrocers. I'll go down and get it. This terrible business with Antonio is making me behave really strangely!

ROSA *exits.*

LUCIA *is alone. She looks around her. A moment or two passes. The telephone rings.* LUCIA *stands there, uncertain. Then she lifts the handset.*

Lucia Hello, who's that? No, she has gone out . . . I am a friend of hers . . . Ah, Professor, it's you . . . Yes, Lucia, that's right, the teacher. How clever of you to recognise me . . . How's it going? What? Who? He's escaped . . .? But how did he manage that, with so many policemen around . . .? Incredible . . .! From the laundry . . . and the coat . . . his coat? I am sorry . . . No, he hasn't come here, I assure you, I'd tell you, Doctor . . . Don't worry, if he turns up, I shall telephone you . . . Alright, yes, yes, without anyone noticing . . . Goodbye, Professor.

She puts down the phone. Behind her, enter ANTONIO, *the real* ANTONIO. *He is wearing a leather coat which is coming apart at the seams. He looks pretty rough.*

Antonio Oh, Lucia, thank goodness I've found you!

Lucia Antonio . . . What the hell are you doing here, have you gone mad? What's come over you?

Antonio Where was I supposed to stick myself? I've been round to your house, but everything was locked up.

Lucia Good God, why aren't you in that basement? It's such a safe spot . . .

Antonio Yes, safe as a grave . . . My grave! No, enough, I can't take any more . . .
for heaven's sake, I want to see people, talk . . . You come and see me
every once in a blue moon . . .

He takes off his coat, and hangs it on the coat rack.

Lucia But try to understand, I can't . . . the police are breathing down my neck
everywhere I go . . . I was scared of leading them to you, and you
getting arrested.

Antonio No way am I going back in there, I don't want to go mad!

Lucia Alright – but you can't stay here. It's dangerous!

Antonio Why dangerous? Who's going to get it into their heads that I'd come and
hide here? I haven't been to Rosa's house in more than a year . . .

Lucia Yes, but all the same, you can't stay . . . Your wife will be back in a minute.

Antonio Well, maybe it's better that way. I shall tell her the whole truth. It's time
to put an end to all this! It's a rotten trick that we're playing on the
poor woman! And I'm paying the price too . . . You have no idea what
it's like, night after night, huddling up every night like an animal, first
with those wrecked cars, and now among all the cockroaches.
Yesterday, I was so desperate, that I caught twenty of them, and put
them in a circle, and with me sitting in the middle, we played at being
the Commission of Inquiry into the Brescia massacre.[8] I'm going mad,
I tell you.

Lucia I know, I know it's not very funny, but be patient, don't give in . . .
particularly not now . . . Just another few days, and . . .

Antonio Lucia, Lucia, it's been months that you've been telling me to be patient:
'Let things calm down, and then we can run off with no problems . . .
Your wife won't cause us any more bother, because she'll have a
husband, even if he is a bit of a mixed-up mess. Then, in a few more
weeks, people will stop talking about Agnelli . . .' No. Every day – it
never stops, newspapers, television, the radio . . . everywhere I go, I see
that face. It's beginning to haunt me! On television they're even
making a multi-part serial about him – the Agnelli Story.

Lucia Alright, it's a bit of a mess. But what do you think you'll achieve by
coming and telling your wife the whole truth and explaining to her that
there are two Antonios? Just when she's convinced herself that the
idiot Agnelli is in fact her Antonio, i.e. you . . . In another few days,
Agnelli will be better, and they'll send him here, and they'll both of
them live happily ever after!

Antonio Agnelli, going to go to bed with my wife?

Lucia Well? What? Don't tell me that you're jealous?

Antonio No! Of course I'm not jealous. But the idea gets right up my nose! He's
screwed me all my life! He pulled the plug on me when he made me
redundant. Then I save his life, and now he's going to be screwing my
wife!

Lucia Antonio, don't be vulgar!

Antonio What do you mean, vulgar! The fact is, he's a bastard! Now they'll grant him a permanent disability pension . . . They'll send him home to live a life of ease . . . in my house . . . and what'll he do? He'll end up with my redundancy money, my life insurance money, my pension and my clarinet no doubt. No, I'm sorry, but I'm going to explain everything.

Lucia Oh brilliant! That way, you'll go straight to prison for at least four years – just on suspicion alone! Do you really think that Rosa will be able to keep her trap shut, even for two minutes?

Antonio Just leave my wife out of this will you.

Enter ROSA, with her shopping bag.

Rosa Here I am . . .

ROSA *sees* ANTONIO. *She stops in her tracks, speechless.* LUCIA *continues, pretending not to have seen her come in.*

Lucia Antonio . . . what do you mean you don't recognise me any longer?! Look at me . . . It's me . . . Lucia!

Rosa Have they sent him home . . .?

Lucia Surely, at least you recognise her, your wife?

ROSA *makes as if to approach* ANTONIO.

No, Rosa, stay there, don't come too close to him . . .

Rosa No. Alright . . . I won't come too close . . . You've healed up really well . . . Your scars hardly show . . .

LUCIA *pushes* ANTONIO *over towards* ROSA.

Lucia Go on, Antonio.

She kicks him furtively on the shins.

Rosa Why did you kick our Antonio?!

Lucia Ah, well, you can't always afford half-measures with psychologically unstable people . . . they'll never get well! Our Professor at the University always used to say: 'A punch and a kick brings a man back to his senses!' Come on, Antonio!

She gives him another kick.

Look, see, it works! Well done . . . Embrace her!

ANTONIO *embraces* ROSA.

Oh God. It did work.

Rosa He's embracing me . . . Oh lord, I'm getting all emotional! I feel weak at the knees . . . Can I embrace him too?

Lucia Yes, Rosa . . . certainly . . .

Rosa Are you sure? Both arms?

Lucia Yes, certainly . . .

ROSA *timidly embraces* ANTONIO. *He stands stock-still, embarrassed, but at the same time moved by the situation.*

Rosa Hello . . . how are you feeling Antonio? Do you recognise me . . .? Who am I . . .? Who am I . . .?

Antonio You are Rosa, you are my wife . . .

Rosa His voice has come back to normal and he recognises me! Now then. Concentrate. Now who is she? Come on!

She kicks his leg, hard.

Antonio Stop it! Let's not carry on with this charade! Listen, it's time you knew what's really going on.

Lucia Stop it, Antonio, don't be stupid!

Rosa Give him another kick to calm him down!

She gives him another kick. LUCIA *does likewise.*

Antonio Ouch . . . stop it!

Rosa We're only doing it for your own good: a punch and a kick brings a man back to his senses.

Antonio I want to tell you what happened.

Lucia Stop it . . . shut up a minute . . .

The window enters, from stage right. It stops centre-stage, LUCIA *goes over to it and looks down onto the road.*

There's no time to lose, Antonio. You're going to have to scram.

Antonio Why? What's going on?

Lucia I might be mistaken, but there's something strange going on down in the street. I bet it's those people from the hospital, coming to get you . . .

She goes to the coat rack and takes down ANTONIO's *jacket.*

Rosa Ah, so they didn't let him out, then?

Lucia No, he escaped. A short while before he arrived, the Doctor telephoned to know whether, by chance, he had come to hide here, in your house . . .

Antonio It's not true, it's a pack of lies, don't believe her. She's just saying that because . . .

Lucia I promise you, listen . . . let's get out of here . . . let's go to my house, while we've still got time . . .

She gives him his jacket.

Antonio No, I'm staying here, till I finish telling Rosa everything. (*He puts his jacket on the table*)

Rosa Sit down! Bitch! With that excuse about how the people are coming to take him away . . . you were just trying to steal my husband again!

The door bursts open. Enter the two POLICEMEN, *followed by the*

INSPECTOR; *the* DOCTOR *is also with them. The window exits, stage right.*

Inspector Here he is! What did I tell you, Professor? I was sure that we'd find him at his wife's house!

Lucia I suppose you're happy now! And I'm a liar!?

Rosa Oh, please, don't hurt him, don't frighten him, he's sick . . .

Inspector Who wants to frighten him? We're among friends, isn't that right, Antonio?

Doctor You had us worried, you know . . . How are you? Your pulse rate is a bit high. What you need is a sedative . . .

Inspector I don't know about sedatives . . .! This one's playing the fool, and making us waste a lot of time! I know what our little Antonio could do with really!

Antonio But who are you . . . I don't even know you!

Rosa You see? Carrying on like that, you've made him lose his memory again . . . To think, up to a moment ago, he recognised everybody. It was a pleasure to see . . .

Policeman Inspector, what shall we do, shall we put handcuffs on him?

Inspector No, it's not necessary . . .

Doctor Give me a hand.

He goes to the table and pulls out of his bag the necessaries for performing an injection.

Antonio Inspector, eh? Listen, I would like to tell you something . . . Listen, because I am going to tell you . . .

Lucia Antonio, are you mad?

Antonio Shut up, you! Inspector, listen to me.

ANTONIO *speaks excitedly with the* INSPECTOR. *He has his back to the* DOCTOR. *The* DOCTOR *comes creeping up on him, in order to give him an injection. But* ANTONIO *and the* INSPECTOR *suddenly contrive to switch positions, and the* INSPECTOR *ends up getting the needle in his own backside.*

Inspector Aagh!

Doctor Oh, excuse me. It's a sedative . . .

Antonio Inspector, listen to me . . .

Inspector You are nothing but a troublemaker . . .! Now he's telling me again that he is Agnelli!

Rosa Agnelli?

Doctor (*preparing a second injection*) Yes. Ever since he made that unfortunate visit to Fiat, he's got it into his head that he is Mr Agnelli!

Rosa Oh, that's all we need!

Doctor It's nothing to be alarmed at – it's the classic split personality phenomenon. Now, come along, take your trousers down . . .

Antonio My trousers?
Doctor It's for the sedative . . .

> *The* DOCTOR *is about to perform the injection, but continues talking with* ROSA.
>
> In these past few months, when he's been confined to his bed, all in plaster, as if he was in a trap . . . he's been chewing over his hatred towards the person who, in his opinion, is responsible for his tragedy . . . in other words, Agnelli.
>
> *Turning to one of the* POLICEMEN:
>
> Oh forget it! Just lift up his jacket . . . (*To* ROSA) . . . and he had ended up identifying with him.
>
> ANTONIO *once again succeeds in transposing the* INSPECTOR, *who receives yet another injection in the backside.*

Inspector Aaaargh!
Doctor Oh, don't be such a cry baby, it's only a little prick.

> *At this point, the* ACTORS *pretend to make a slip-up on stage. The* DOCTOR *pretends to trip, and loses his hypodermic syringe. The* ACTRESS *playing* ROSA *looks disconcerted as she pickes up the syringe. The* ACTORS *burst out laughing. The* ACTOR *playing the* DOCTOR *feigns embarrassment and consternation. The* ACTOR *playing the part of* ANTONIO *speaks.*

Actor playing the part of Antonio Well, there you are, it could have happened to anybody . . . particularly to real doctors! But anyway, it's my fault, because I spun him round too fast. It's my fault. Doctors, as we know are never responsible, either in civil or in criminal law. OK, let's start again where we left off . . .
Doctor (*Makes as if to start again, but breaks into confused laughter*) Hold his jacket up . . .
Antonio Don't be embarrassed, Professor . . .
Doctor You, hold his jacket up . . . and he had ended up identifying with him.
Rosa Oh heavens, he's identified with him, with Agnelli, and he's getting a split personality . . . Like Dr Jekyll, who at the start was . . . and then became . . . and so, when he doesn't recognise me, it's because he's convinced that he is Agnelli.
Doctor Ten out of ten!

> *The* DOCTOR *prepares a third injection.* ANTONIO *is in deep conversation with the* INSPECTOR, *who by now is reeling from the injections.*

Inspector Excuse me, Doctor, come over here a moment. Now he's saying that he was the one who saved Agnelli. I don't know about split personalities, this one's just trying to make idiots out of all of us!

ANTONIO *takes advantage of a momentary lack of attention by the guards. He makes a dash for the door. He goes out, and locks it behind him, as he runs off. In order to escape, he has to shift one of the* POLICEMEN. *The* POLICEMAN *ends up getting the injection that was meant for* ANTONIO.

Policeman Aaaargh! He's escaped!

Inspector Don't stand there like a dummy?! Get after him, quick!

Policeman He's locked us in . . . The key was on the outside!

Inspector Well then, shoot the lock off!

Rosa No, please, don't shoot the door down . . . I've got another key. Wait a minute, I'll find it . . .

Inspector No, there's no time . . . Fire! Fire! Fire!

The POLICEMEN *fire* – BANG BANG.

From outside the door, we hear a stifled scream.

A musical interlude follows, during which everyone freezes for a moment.

Rosa Antonio! Antonio was behind that door! You've killed him . . .!

The door swings open. After a moment, enter the EXAMINING MAGISTRATE.

Examining Magistrate My leg . . . There's a hole in my leg . . . Why did you shoot me?

Inspector Your Honour! What on earth were you doing behind the door?

Examining Magistrate I was knocking . . . But do you always shoot people when they knock at the door? (*He falls to the floor*)

Inspector Hurry up, Doctor . . . he's passed out . . . And you, could you help too.

Doctor Don't worry. Amputation is my favourite.

Inspector Look, if anybody lets slip a word about this incident, I'll kill them! If it ends up in the newspapers – magistrate kneecapped by the Police . . .' – I'll top myself!

Exit the POLICEMEN, *the* INSPECTOR, *the* DOCTOR *and* LUCIA, *carrying the* EXAMINING MAGISTRATE. ROSA *remains on stage. She is dazed and bemused by what has happened. She closes the door, and looks at the wrecked lock.*

Rosa Madness! Nobody's going to believe me if I tell them! Did you see that? Nasty habit they've got, of pulling out their guns at the slightest provocation . . .

The window whizzes on stage. ROSA *looks through it.*

Poor Antonio . . . Let's hope they're not going to shoot him too . . . Oh God, there he is . . . That's him, hiding behind the bus . . . No, he's gone . . . Maybe it wasn't him . . .

ROSA *goes to the table, where* ANTONIO*'s car coat is still lying.*

Oh I hope they don't take him back to that hospital because then he really will go barmy sharing a split personality with Dr Jekyll, who's half beast and half Agnelli. Well it's the same thing really . . . Hey, but here's his coat . . . He went off without a coat . . . he's bound to catch cold . . .

ROSA *takes* ANTONIO*'s coat and goes to hang it on the coat rack. The door opens. Enter the* DOUBLE. *He is wearing an overcoat. His head is wrapped in a long scarf. As the* DOUBLE *enters, the window leaves the stage.*

Double Excuse me

Rosa Antonio! You've given them the slip . . . it's you . . . you got away . . . you made it!

Double Maaay . . . I . . . cooome . . . iiin. Is aaaaanyone in?

Rosa Yes, no-one's in . . . they've all gone off to take a gentleman to hospital, because he knocked at the door and they shot him in the leg . . . so as to open the door . . . and then he turned out to be an Examining Magistrate.

Double Iiiii've . . . gooooot . . . awaaaay!

Rosa Yes, I know!

Double Thaaat . . . creeetin of an Inspeeector . . . is convinced that I kiiidnapped myself . . . an autoterrorist!

Rosa Calm down, Antonio, slow down and get your breath back . . . All that running that you've been doing, your scars are beginning to show again . . . They've all swollen up with the fright . . . Look how you're sweating . . . Are you thirsty. Would you like something to drink?

Double Yes, please, a little non-carbonated mineral water . . . because otherwise I'll burp, and I'll blow my nose . . . off . . .

The DOUBLE *takes off his coat and goes over to the coat rack.*

Rosa, OK, I'll bring it at once. (*Notices the overcoat*) But what are you doing with a coat on?

Double It's cold!

Rosa Did you have two overcoats?

Double No, this one's a long jacket . . .

Rosa This doubling-up of yours is beginning to be obsessive . . .

Double Listen, madam. I have to tell you something . . . which obviously you are not aware of . . .

Rosa But now you're calling me madam . . .?!

Double Madam, I do not know you . . . I am not your husband . . .

Rosa Yes, dear, calm down . . . sit down . . . Now you just drink your non-carbonated mineral water, and try not to talk nonsense . . .

ROSA *goes into the kitchen, and after a moment returns with a bottle and a glass.*

Double But madam, I am not talking nonsense at all! I have never been so lucid and self-aware!

From the plastic bag that he has with him, the DOUBLE *pulls out a funnel.*

Rosa Jesus Christ! Well, why don't you show it, and stop calling me madam!

Double Alright, I'll stop calling you madam. Would you be so kind as to help me to screw the funnel into the tube . . . (*He fiddles with the funnel*) No . . . it's alright, I've done it.

Rosa The funnel? What for?

Double So as to drink.

Rosa You drink through your neck?

Double Yes . . . I can't yet drink through my throat . . . until the scar tissues heal up completely on my glottis and epiglottis . . . Ah . . . It's cold! Just pour it straight out of the bottle. It's more convenient.

ROSA does as he says.

Rosa Oh Lord, what am I seeing – my husband, with a funnel stuck in him. You look like a bloody beer barrel!

Double And now, will you please sit down, because I want to tell you my story . . . the real story

Rosa Alright – tell me.

Double After the accident, for months it was as if I had disappeared . . .

Rosa Yes, I know . . .

Double Then, that day when they took me to the assembly line at the Mirafiori plant, it was as if a bomb had exploded in my brain: 50,000 electric shock treatments all in one go! All of a sudden, I remembered who I was. That I was Agnelli, and that I didn't want anything to do with the shit and the mess and the grime. And now there I was, I . . . Agnelli, hooked up with a welding gun which was spitting blinding sparks all over the place, and I started trembling as if I had a 220 volt plug up my arse . . .

Rosa Calm down, Antonio . . .

Double I am not Antonio! I am not some stupid worker who starts trembling! I am above everything, I am! They think that I have been kidnapped . . . but no, I have only been swapped! And look at me now, with this loony puppet's face! The face of one of my lineworkers . . . what a humiliating joke!

Rosa Listen, Dr Jekyll . . . will you stop that? I've had it up to here, with all these split personality changes! Either you calm down, or I'll break your legs! (*She kicks him*)

Double Aaargh! Are you mad?!

We hear the sound of a police siren. Enter the window, from stage right. ROSA looks out through the window.

Is that the police?! Are they arriving?

Rosa No, it's not them. They're not stopping. But at the same time, it's not a very
clever idea for you to wait here until they do turn up and arrest you . . .
Let's go up in the loft . . . Take your scarf, for your scars . . .
I've got it all fixed up, you see. You can even sleep there; I set it all up so
as to rent it to a student. Come on, come on, I'll show you up there. I've
had a water tap put in, too.

They exit. We hear ROSA's *voice disappearing off upstairs.*

Remember to watch out for the steps, they're a bit steep. Nobody knows
that this room is here, because I've not yet reported it to the authorities.
There you are, come in. Look I've had electric light put in too.

Then the hall door opens, and ANTONIO *the worker enters.*

Antonio Rosa! Are you there, Rosa? Anyone in? Well, thank goodness, they've
all gone away, and let's hope that they all leave me in peace. Look how
I'm sweating! I'm soaked!

*He removes his jacket and shirt, and throws them on the floor in the
middle of the room.*

I wonder if Rosa's got a clean jumper for me to change into.

He exits via the centre door. Enter ROSA. *She stands by the door for a
moment, speaking to the* DOUBLE *upstairs:*

Rosa Now you stay there and behave. Don't make any noise. I'll bring you some
food in a moment. (*She goes towards the kitchen*) Goodness, I'm all
emotions . . .! I'd never have expected to get so emotional, having my
husband back home! I'm all worked up. I'm really all worked up . . .!
(*She sees his clothes thrown in the middle of the floor*) That shows how
worked up I am! I didn't even notice that he'd taken his clothes off (*She
picks up his clothes*) And he's dumped them all here on the floor, just as
he always used to . . . Oh, how pleased I am to have him back . . . how
happy I am to have his nice dirty shirts to wash . . . and iron . . . and to
cook for him, slaving like a skivvy . . . that's living for you!

ROSA *exits into the kitchen. She is radiant with happiness.* ANTONIO
*re-enters. He has put on a clean jumper. He is drying his head and arms
with a towel.*

Antonio Rosa, are you back . . . are you back?
Rosa Why are you back here? Is something wrong? Why have you come back?
Antonio Ah, why, shouldn't I have come back? I suppose you'd rather I let myself
be locked up like a poor sod, for the rest of my life?
Rosa But what do you mean, 'the rest of your life . . .?' Just a day or two, until
things sort themselves out.
Antonio No. If I go inside, I'll never come out again. I could be inside for twelve
years . . .

Rosa Don't say silly things . . . You don't think I'll be keeping you up there for
twelve years . . .

Antonio Up where? What do you mean, up there? Rosa, what are you raving on
about?

Rosa (*Thinks that her husband does not remember having been upstairs*) Look,
nothing is going right around here . . . I am beginning to lose patience.
Look, if you don't get yourself sorted out, I . . . I am going to pour
twelve pints of bromide down the hole in your neck!

She takes the funnel and points it meaningfully at ANTONIO.

You're driving everybody nuts! First things are black, then they're
white, then you change your mind, and you don't even remember!!!
Come on, up into the loft, do as I say!

Antonio In the loft? Why in the loft?

Rosa Because it's a safe hiding place!

Antonio No, it's not safe at all. The loft has no way out, it's a trap. If you don't
mind, I would prefer to stay over there; in the other room. (*He points
towards the bedroom*) Because that leads onto the terrace, and so, if
they come looking for me, I'll be able to get away over the roofs . . .

Rosa You'll fall off and end up in bits . . . and then we'll start all over again!
Bruuu . . . braaa . . . bray . . . astronaut! astronaut! But do what you
want!

Antonio Rosa, who's this astronaut?

Rosa Stop it! Do what you like. It's impossible to reason with you. I'm going to
get you something to eat.

ROSA *goes into the kitchen.*

Antonio At last you've said something intelligent. I'm starving!

*He notices that there are two coats hanging on the coatrack: the one
belonging to him, and the other to the* DOUBLE.

ROSA *re-enters, bringing bread, glasses, a bottle of wine, plates, cutlery
and serviettes. She goes to the table and starts to lay it.*

Rosa You're very lucky, you know. Today I prepared the stew for the whole
week, with a pig's trotter . . .

Antonio (*Lifting off the* DOUBLE's *overcoat*) Whose is it?

Rosa The pig's trotter? It's ours . . . we'll eat it.

Antonio (*Goes over to* ROSA *with the two coats*) I'm talking about the coat.
Whose is it?

Rosa It's yours. Whose do you expect it to be?

Antonio My one is that one – so whose one is this one? The astronaut's?

Rosa It's yours!

Antonio Rosa, who is this astronaut who leaves coats all over the place . . .?

Rosa You can pack that in! It's yours. You had two of them, one on top of the
other! Two overcoats! You were going round with two overcoats!

Antonio Me? I had two overcoats, one on top of the other! I was going round with
two overcoats! . . . one on top of the other!!
Rosa Yes, you!

> ROSA *picks up a chair and is about to throw it at him.* ANTONIO
> *addresses her extremely calmly, as if trying to deal with a raving loony.*

Antonio Of course. (*Points to his leather carcoat*) And I suppose this was my
waistcoat!
Rosa (*Going back to the table*) So. Shall I heat it up?
Antonio What? The coat?
Rosa No, the stew! You know very well I meant the stew. How are you going to
eat this stew . . .?

> ANTONIO *looks at her in increasing amazement. Then, thinking that*
> ROSA *has gone completely round the twist, he moves slowly to the door to*
> *make a getaway.*

Rosa No, seriously, how do you do it? How do you swallow? Do you suck it
down through the funnel? Or through the tube in your neck? And how
are we going to get it down . . . There's no way it'll go through . . . even
if I push it, because even if I cut the meat up into little bits, it's still
going to be too big . . . and since it mustn't touch your glottis, or your
epiglottis . . . which, incidentally, are two words that I have never heard
of . . . then how are you going to eat? Will you be sucking it down, or
not? But then, it won't go through the tube in your neck . . . it won't go
through!

> *Only now does she notice that* ANTONIO *is about to leave the room.*

Antonio Yes, carry on . . . you're quite right . . . Carry on just like that. Perfect!
When it doesn't pass via the glottis . . . the tube is the best way . . . suck it
though the funnel . . . the funnel is designed especially for sucking . . . and
as for me, my glottis . . . you know . . . and then also my epiglottis . . .
Rosa Where are you going? This is no laughing matter . . . Come over here . . .
Antonio Yes, yes . . . Hang on a minute. I'm going out for a moment to get my
third overcoat, which I left downstairs . . . I had three coats, you know!
Rosa Careful . . . somebody's coming . . . Quick, go into the bedroom . . .

> ANTONIO *scrambles into the bedroom.*

> I'll lock you in . . . I'll give it two turns of the key. (*She does as she says*)
> . . . and you stay quiet . . .
Antonio Yes . . . who is it?
Rosa For God's sake shut up. (*She goes to the door and peeps out*) Yes? Oh it's you
. . . and you.

> *She shuts the door again, runs to the centre door, and without re-opening*
> *it, shouts:*

Don't worry, it wasn't anyone . . . it's next-door . . . I don't like him at all, a right Peeping Tom . . .! The minute he hears a noise he comes out nosy parkering . . . I can't stand the man . . . I'm . . . I'm going to report him . . . I'll report him for 'unnatural curiosity'!

ROSA *goes out into the kitchen. No sooner has she gone than the* DOUBLE *appears round the front door.*

Double Rosa, can I come in? Am I bothering you?
Rosa Be patient for a moment! I'm dishing out the stew. I'll be there to open the door in a moment.
Double Oh, there's no need to bother. I'll let myself in.

ROSA *enters, with a saucepan brimful of stew. She stares at him, dumbfounded.*

Rosa But how did you get in?
Double Through the door, why?
Rosa But it was locked!
Double No, it wasn't locked!
Rosa How stupid of me, obviously, as I was turning the key a moment ago . . .

We hear the wail of a siren. The window whizzes onstage. ROSA *rushes over and looks down into the street.*

There they are again . . . Oh no, it's an ambulance, it's not stopping . . .
Double The police!
Rosa Yes, but they're not stopping . . . Oh, what a life this is! Sweet, I would like so much for the two of us, me and you, to sit here, nice and comfortable, and eat, but it's too dangerous. Listen, let's take the plates and the cutlery, and go into the room . . .
Double Oh no, please. I can't stand it. When I'm in there, I get ghastly nightmares, like in the hospital, I want to be sick . . . I can't hold my food down . . .
Rosa Alright, let's take a chance,

The DOUBLE *sits at the table.*

but at the slightest suspicious noise, you'll have to disappear. Here you are, help yourself.

She passes him the stewpot, and then goes over to the sideboard where she takes two jars and brings them over to the DOUBLE.

Look, I've bought you some Cremona mustard too, and there's some green sauce . . .

Double But Rosa, this is boiled beef . . .
Rosa Yes?
Double and Rosa Yes?

Double And boiled sausage . . . and even a boiled pig's foot . . .
Rosa Yes?!! . . .
Double Everything boiled . . .

ROSA *is about to lose her grip on herself.*

Rosa Yes? So? Is something wrong? Changed your mind yet again?
Double No, I really like stew . . . it's just that you've forgotten that my tube is very
thin, and the food won't go through the funnel . . . particularly a
sausage that size . . .
Rosa We've been through this before haven't we? I could mince it . . . But even
then, it's too big to go through that little hole!
Double It won't go through the hole in my neck, but it will go through my nose!
Rosa You eat stew through your nose?!
Double Yes. In hospital they even made me suck spaghetti up through my nose
. . . the bolognese sauce made a terrible mess . . . Now I'll show you a
little gadget that I've brought with me from the hospital . . .

From his plastic bag he pulls out a kind of mask.

There, you see, these tubes go up into the nostrils. Here you connect
the output socket from a meat mincer. I had a really good one in
hospital, electric . . . But I forgot it in the rush.
Rosa Oh, how stupid of me, I've got a mincing machine too, but it's one of those
old ones, with the handle that you turn.

She goes over to the sideboard to get it.

Double Let's have a look. The important thing is that the back end has to be the
same diameter. Perfect! Size 12!
Rosa Incredible! Antonio . . . even the colour matches!!
Double Now I'll show you how it works. There, you see, first you put on the mask
like this. Then you put the tubes up your nostrils, and then you put the
meatgrinder here, on your head . . .

He suddenly takes the mask off again.

Oh goodness, look . . .
Rosa What's up, Antonio?
Double The meat grinder grinding on my head, I feel as if my brain's being
ground up . . . Have you got any cords?
Rosa Cords?
Double Yes cords. To tie me down.
Rosa Tie you down?
Double Yes. Otherwise I won't be able to resist the instinct to pull the tubes out of
my nose.
Rosa Well, we could try it with these straps. They're the straps I use for my
suitcases . . .

She pulls some straps out of a drawer.

Double Perfect! And this armchair with the arms is tailor-made.

He arranges a couple of straps on each arm of the armchair.

And with this one, you can tie my neck back against the upright part, like this!

Rosa Oh, it's horrible – you look as if you're in an electric chair!

Double You said it! I am in the electric chair. Rosa, you're going to have to be strong. Please, Rosa, don't be swayed if, at the beginning, I plead with you to set me free. You must be strong, you must make me eat at any cost!

Rosa Yes, indeed, at any cost! I shall be very strict. I shall make you eat everything!

The phone rings.

Oh God, the phone . . . I can't answer . . . I'm crying . . .

She answers the phone in a perfectly normal voice.

Hello, yes Professor, it's me. No, I've not seen Antonio. No, no, I assure you, he hasn't been here. I would tell you, Professor. I wouldn't say a word to the Inspector – he's so uncouth – but I would tell *you*! Please, let me know if anything happens. I'm in agony here! Goodbye. (*She puts the phone down again*)

Double What did he say?

The DOUBLE *has arranged the straps around the arms of the armchair.*

Rosa It was the Professor . . . If you ask me, he wasn't taken in. They'll be here any minute. Quick, let's take everything upstairs, into the other room . . .

Double No, for heaven's sake, don't you understand – I can't wait any longer – I'm dying of hunger! Rosa, you've got to grind some stew up my nose, or I shall go mad!

Rosa I'll grind for you in a couple of minutes . . . Go on up, I'll join you. Take the bottle of wine, and the glasses.

Double Bread, I want bread . . .(*He makes a dive for the bread basket*)

Rosa Leave the bread alone . . .

Double But without bread I won't be able to eat the stew . . .

Rosa I've got grated breadcrumbs . . . Go on up . . . I'll bring the rest up, including the electric chair. (*She runs into the kitchen*) Hurry up!

Double Alright. I'll wait for you. But you get a move on.

The DOUBLE *exits via the door leading to the hall landing.* ROSA *calls out from the kitchen:*

Rosa Just a moment, I'll turn off the gas. I've got some fruit down here. Afterwards I'll make you a fruit salad.

She re-enters, goes over to the table, and puts the plates, cutlery and the stewpot etc. onto the armchair.

Imagine, what a shame, having to mince up such a good bit of beef, as if it was meat for meatballs . . .

ANTONIO *the worker calls from the bedroom.*

Antonio Rosa, can we get a move on – I'm still here, waiting!

Rosa Don't be so impatient! What am I supposed to do? Sprout wings? I'm loading up the electric chair!

Antonio Loading what? Rosa, what nonsense are you talking now?

Rosa Hurry up and give me a hand . . . I can't manage it . . . it's too heavy . . .

Antonio Alright. Just come and unlock the door . . .

Rosa It's open! Push it and see.

Antonio Don't talk rubbish, Rosa . . . It's locked, solid!

ROSA *looks at the door, speechless. Then she goes to the bedroom door and turns the key. Re-enter* ANTONIO.

Where have you been?

ROSA *looks at him, bewildered.*

Rosa Antonio, please, you're going to have to explain to me how you managed to go into the bedroom, lock yourself in, and still leave the key on the outside of the door . . .!

Antonio What did I do?

Rosa You locked yourself in the bedroom, with two turns of the key!

Antonio I did? It was you, you who locked me in with two turns of the key.

Rosa Yes, but that was before. But then you got out!

Antonio I got out?

Rosa Yes!

Antonio How?

Rosa Through the door! How else?

Antonio I came out by the door?

Rosa Yeees!!!

Antonio When?

Rosa Before!

Antonio Don't talk rubbish!

ROSA *picks up a chair and makes as if to throw it at him.*

Rosa You did come out! You did come out!

Antonio It's true! I was trying to keep it a secret from you, but obviously I failed. (*He mimes everything that follows*) I got out by using an old trick that we use at the Mirafiori factory. The foremen lock us in, so we get out by sticking our hands under the door . . . Of course, at first we stick them, i.e. our hands, under a stamping press . . . so as to squash them flat a bit . . . Then we stick our hands under the door, and push them through as far as the elbow . . . Then we give a little twist, so as to get the knobbly bits through more easily . . . until we get our arms through as well, right up to the shoulder. Then we grab the key. But the key is too thick, it won't go under the door! So, we stick our heads under the door, and push . . . and push . . . and whoops! That's how we get out. Are you happy now? They call me the Scarlet Pimpernel!

ROSA *listens to him in blank amazement. As* ANTONIO *finishes speaking, she removes the scarf from round her neck, and wraps it round her head.*

Alright? Rosa, Rosa, what are you doing, Rosa?

Rosa I've got a headache!

Antonio Well maybe if we sit down to eat, maybe it'll go . . .

Without answering, ROSA *goes over to the electric chair. She looks at* ANTONIO *meaningfully.* ANTONIO *does not understand.*

Now you're talking

Rosa (*Persuasively, talking as if to a mad person*) The electric chair . . . come on . . . let's go into the bedroom, and I'll grind for you . . . I shall be ruthless . . . down to the last particle of meat . . .

Antonio Stooop it! You're driving me mad! It's a trick, to drive me out of my mind! Stoooop it!

Rosa I shall do my duty! In spite of everything that's happened! Antonio, let's go in there!

Antonio In where?

Rosa Into the bedroom . . .!

Antonio To do what?

Rosa To eat!

Antonio Noooo!!! For months I've been eating like a wretch. Now, just once, I want to eat here, sitting down like a good Christian . . . A Christian, and a Marxist! Sitting down! A Marxist Christian, sitting down . . . and slightly puzzled . . . because of what's happened in Poland!

During this speech, ROSA *slips slowly to the floor. She curls up in a heap, with her head resting on the floor, and stays there, silent, as if crushed.*

What's up now? What are you doing, Rosa . . .? Rosa, I know where you've been all this time . . .? You've become a hippy haven't you? Were you in a commune? And who was your guru? The astronaut?!

Rosa Antonio, I am very confused . . .! Antonio, we must go in there, into the other room . . .

Antonio What, like that? Crawling along the floor?

Rosa . . . because if the police arrive . . .

The window zooms in. ROSA *shouts at it.*

. . . I said 'if' the police arrive!

The window takes fright, and rushes back into the wings.

Antonio Who cares! Lock the door, and put the chain on! (*He sits down at the table*) You know that door chain I had put in specially. And if the police want to get past that, they'll have to batter the door down.

ROSA *picks herself up off the floor, and goes to lock the door with the door chain.*

And while they're battering the door down, I'll be eating this wonderful stew!

He clears the armchair off, putting the various objects on the table. He sits down, holding the stewpot.

I've said before and I'll say it again, Rosa, that nobody in the whole world makes stew the way that you do . . .

ROSA *desperately tries to hold back her tears.*

Rosa Yes, I know you've said it before.

Antonio I could eat this with my eyeballs!

Rosa And instead you're going to have to eat it with your nose!

She goes up to ANTONIO *and straps his hands to the arms of the armchair.*

Antonio Rosa? Rosa! What are you doing? Why are you strapping me down?

Rosa To make you eat, right?

Antonio Rosa, please, afterwards we'll have time to talk, and you can tell me all about the customs in your commune. Not now, though . . .

Rosa Stop it! Let's start with a nice bit of broth . . . just to whet your appetite . . . But . . . Antonio, how are you going to eat it?

Antonio I won't eat it, I'll drink it . . .

Rosa But do you want it down your neck, or are you going to suck it up your nose . . . ? How would you prefer it? It would be better through the neck. (*She picks up the funnel*) Let's hope I manage to find the hole . . .! (*She sticks the funnel down his neck*)

Antonio You've punched a hole in my shoulderblade! Please . . . untie me . . .

ROSA *ignores his pleas. She puts a strap round his neck, pulling his head back against the upright of the armchair.*

Rosa, please . . . Rosa, it's true, I've been a louse . . . Rosa, I've treated you badly, I've been like a son of a bitch . . . I've not respected you . . . But you must be generous . . . and forgive me. I'll come back to you, Rosa! Please, let me go!

Rosa My sweet, my sweet . . .

Antonio Forgive me, Rosa. I love you, Rosa!

Rosa How long have I waited to hear you say those words!

Antonio Rosa . . .

Rosa I love you too . . .!

She picks up the mask from the table, and fits it on his head. She pushes the tubes up his nose. As ANTONIO speaks, ROSA adjusts the mask to get a tight fit.

Antonio Rosa, Rosa . . . my nostrils are all blocked up . . . I've got something up my nose . . . Rosa, I feel like an elephant . . . Why do you go to see those kind of films . . . You know that they only give you ideas!

Rosa Ssssh – keep quiet . . .

Antonio That's enough, now, Rosa . . . Let me go . . . Help! Help!!

Rosa Antonio, don't shout like that . . .

Antonio Heeeelp!!

Rosa Antonio, don't shout! Don't you realise that you're torturing me! (*She completes the operation of fitting the machine*)

Antonio No, you're torturing me! Help . . . Help . . .!

ANTONIO's shout transforms into the trumpeting of an elephant.

Rosa Antonio, stop it . . . Antonio . . . Stop pretending to be an elephant . . . What will the neighbours say? . . . Stop it!

ANTONIO carries on howling.

Shut up!

ROSA no longer knows what to do to shut him up: in desperation she shoves a serviette into his mouth.

Stop it! You must eat. Keep quiet!

ANTONIO continues howling but slowly his howls are transformed into the sound of a steamboat siren.

Antonio, stop that! The neighbours will hear . . . Stop it! I won't have you being a steamboat! Oh my God, he's turning puce . . . Oh, how stupid of me, I've blocked up all his holes . . . So how's he going to breathe . . .?
What shall I put in place of the serviette? Ah yes, your favourite clarinet . . .

The clarinet is hanging from a standard lamp. ROSA picks up the whole caboodle, and puts it in front of ANTONIO.

We'll leave it hanging from the lamp, so that you can breathe, and play at the same time, if you want! Out and in.

She takes the serviette out of his mouth, and inserts the clarinet's mouthpiece. ANTONIO moves the fingers of his right hand up and down the keys of the clarinet, which gives out a blues sequence of high and low notes, commenting grotesquely on the situation.

Now I can give you your broth . . .

She pours the broth down the funnel.

Don't worry, it's not hot . . . I've put some grated cheese in, and a couple of drops of lemon to knock out the grease . . . There, that's goood . . . swallow it down, it'll do you good . . . but . . . but . . . what's this – you're doing a wee?? Oh no . . . it's the soup running out of your trousers . . . I must have missed the hole with the tube! Oh well, too bad. Let's get on with the stew. Let's start with this nice bit of rump . . .

ROSA *takes some pieces of meat and puts them into the meatgrinder. The clarinet's wailing transforms into a desperate rock rhythm.* ROSA, *unperturbed, continues grinding, turning the handle of the mincer. There is a loud knocking at the door. From outside the door, the* INSPECTOR *shouts:*

Inspector Open up! Police! Open up, or we'll knock the door down!!
Rosa There they are! I told you that they'd be back . . . Keep quiet, don't budge.

ANTONIO *lets out a groan, through the clarinet.*

Rosa Keep quiet!

With a big crash, the door bursts open, under the weight of the two POLICEMEN. ROSA *continues turning the handle of the mincer, unperturbed.* ANTONIO *plays the clarinet with increasing desperation. The* INSPECTOR *and the* POLICEMEN *stare at the scene in amazement.*

Inspector But what on earth are you doing?
Rosa I'm feeding my husband.
Inspector With a clarinet in his mouth?
Rosa Yes it's the only way he'll eat! Would you mind giving me a hand. Carry on grinding up his meat. I'll go and prepare him a nice fruit salad . . . But don't let yourself feel sorry for him, if he asks you to unstrap him . . . He must eat: it's a matter of life and death!

ROSA *goes into the kitchen. One of the* POLICEMEN *removes the clarinet from* ANTONIO'*s mouth.*

Antonio Help . . . I've got a bit of boiled sausage up my nose . . . Have you got a nose-pick!
Inspector What are you babbling about?
Antonio Help! Set me free! That woman's a horror! Take me away from here . . .
Inspector Take you away where? To prison, perhaps?
Antonio To the zoo if you like . . . Just get me away from here. That woman is mad! She's killing me, sausage by sausage!
Inspector Alright . . . we'll set you free, if you do us a little favour. You're going to tell us a few details about the Agnelli kidnap. You were there, weren't you, that evening, on the embankment?

Antonio Yes, certainly I was there, on the embankment . . .
Inspector Very good!
Antonio But I had nothing to do with the kidnap. In fact, it was me who saved
Agnelli . . .
Inspector Give the handle a little twirl!

The POLICEMAN *does as he says.*

Antonio No, no! Stop it! Yes, it's true . . . I confess! I am the head of the armed
gang that kidnapped Agnelli!

The POLICEMAN *stops turning the handle.*

I'll tell all . . . I'll spill the beans . . . just set me free!
Inspector What a wonderful little machine! We ought to have a little gadget like
this down at the nick!

The POLICEMEN *set* ANTONIO *free.*

ROSA *enters, carrying a soup tureen.*

Rosa I've made some fruit salad for you.

ANTONIO *leaps from his seat and runs to seek protection among the*
POLICEMEN.

Antonio No, no not the fruit salad, get me out of here!
Rosa But why did you set him free?
Inspector Don't worry, madam . . . we're just taking him down to HQ with us for
a while . . . He's got a few little things to get off his chest . . . Now you
just sit down there, eat your fruit salad, and keep your mouth shut!
Let's go, let's go.

ANTONIO *exits, with the* POLICEMEN.

Rosa Oh, Antonio! Inspector, where are you taking him? Wait, his tubes . . . and
the meatgrinder . . .
Inspector No thank you. We use less sophisticated methods down at the station.

The INSPECTOR *exits.* ROSA *is beside herself.*

Rosa Oh God. Poor Antonio, what a terrible thing to happen! But why on earth
are they taking him to the police station . . .?

Enter the window. ROSA *looks out of it.*

Poor Antonio . . . There he is . . . they're loading him into the wagon . . .
Antonio . . . Antoniooo . . .

The DOUBLE *enters again, via the door, which is still wide open.*

Double Yes?
Rosa He answered me! Antonioooo!

Double I'm here . . . No need to shout! Since you took so long coming up, I came down. Now, please, hurry up with that food . . . I'm dying of hunger . . .

Rosa Oh God . . . one Antonio here, and another Antonio there . . . Two Antonios . . .!! Your personality's completely split in two!

> ROSA *crashes to the floor. The* DOUBLE *wanders over to the window and looks out.*

Double Ah yes . . . One Antonio here, one Antonio there . . . If I can find a third one . . . I'll be God!

BLACKOUT

MUSICAL INTERLUDE

ACT II

Scene 2

We are still in ROSA's *house. As the lights come up, there is nobody on stage. The bedroom door opens. A character appears, wearing a leather jacket full of pockets and zips. He wears a commando-style woollen beret, with motor cycle dark glasses, a knife down his boot, and a big pistol in his holster.*

He sneaks along the wall, and looks under the table. He peers into the other rooms. In his hand he has a walkie-talkie, which is making noises: squeaks and whistles. He goes to the window and pulls something off. Then he goes to the coat rack and pulls off a little gadget. He goes to the hall door, opens it and signals to someone to come in.

Another character, almost identical, enters, walking on tiptoe, and followed shortly after by two others, carrying false drawers and shelves in order to disguise the sideboard in which their Group Leader will be hidden with his head inside a false soup tureen.

All this is done ballet-style, to the accompaniment of waltz music. The second AGENT, *assisted by his colleague, pulls the drawers out of the sideboard. The* GROUP LEADER *pulls out a small radio with a long aerial, and talks into it:*

Group Leader Hurry up with the furniture. Hello, hello, 008½ Fellini calling HQ, do you read me? Yes, we are setting up our observation post . . . The woman is still upstairs, talking excitedly with a man in the loft . . . No, it's not her husband. He keeps calling her madam. I don't know who it is . . .

The two assistants have removed the sideboard. They bring on-stage another sideboard, which has been constructed as a kind of stocks, with a big hole, through which the GROUP LEADER *will put his head. On either side there are smaller holes for his hands to go through.*

Group Leader Yes, I've already searched the place, I've located the hidden microphones. No, not our stuff. Must be the f . . . ing anti-terrorist mob . . . Yes; already dealt with . . .

As he continues his report, the GROUP LEADER *is fitted into the sideboard. In a squatting position. The* GROUP LEADER's *head is now disguised with a soup tureen, arranged like an armoured helmet.*

Watch out – they're coming down . . . I'm in position. Over and out!

The sideboard is returned to its original position. One AGENT *climbs into the television, the others exit. At the end of this action, enter* ROSA *and* AGNELLI.

Rosa Ladies and gentlemen. Three days have passed since the last scene. Well if
he can do it so can I. Here, do you know who he is? It's only Gianni
Agnelli, living in Rosa's house. I mean I don't mind looking after your
own but this is ridiculous. I mean he is useless around the house, he
can't even change a plug. He thinks that manual labour is a Spanish
waiter. And there's my Antonio in prison being kicked about by the
police. They think he's a terrorist and Agnelli won't do anything about
it. He's got something cooking in that tiny brain of his and he won't tell
me what it is. Anyway, back to the play . . .

She continues acting, addressing AGNELLI.

. . . in prison, getting kicked about, and it's all your fault!

ROSA *goes over to the sideboard, she opens one of the drawers, and then
closes it, worried.*

Double All my fault?
Rosa Where's my cigarettes . . .!

She opens another drawer, into which the GROUP LEADER *swiftly slips
a packet of cigarettes.*

Double Calm down, please . . . before you say it's 'all my fault'! . . .
Rosa Ah, here they are . . .

ROSA *takes the packet; she takes out a cigarette; she puts the packet
back in the drawer. She turns to look at* AGNELLI *for a moment, and the
drawer shuts of its own accord, pulled in by the* GROUP LEADER.

Double I would like to know, my dear Mrs Rosa, (*He lights* ROSA'*s cigarette with
a match*) if this so very generous Antonio of yours moved so much as a
finger when I was down there at the hospital, having my face rebuilt to
look like his. Did he ever move so much as a finger? No, sir. He didn't
give a damn!

*He lifts the lid off the soup tureen, and throws in the match. He puts the lid
down again, but not before seeing the head of the* GROUP LEADER.

I'm not feeling well today . . .! And then they say that we employers are
cynical! What's this, if it's not cynicism? (*He sees the television*) But
excuse me, speaking of strange things . . . Is it normal to find a
television stuck between the kitchen and the dining-room? Following
you around! What channel are we . . .
Rosa Good God, what a fuss-pot you are! I must have moved it to clean up, and
forgotten to put it back. Anyway, if you don't like your present face,
you can always have it rebuilt just as it was before . . . with the money
you've got . . .
Double Yes, have my face rebuilt! But first of all, I would have to have all my
features dismantled, back to basics . . .

The chest of drawers moves.

Excuse me, is it normal in this house for drawers to move of their own accord? What is this, the commode's revenge? As I was saying . . . in order to rebuild my face, they're going to have to dismantle my present features, and peel me like an apple, from my chin to my forehead. And then, once they've rebuilt my skull, what are they going to cover it with, what kind of skin . . . since they've already stripped my backside as bare as a baboon's bum!

Enter a MAN *in overalls, pushing a dishwashing machine.*

Man Excuse me, don't mind me, does Mrs Berardi live here?

Rosa Yes, that's me – If you don't mind my saying so, do you always come into people's houses without even knocking first?

Man What difference does it make? Even if I had knocked, you wouldn't have suddenly turned into someone else, would you?

Rosa What a comedian!

Man Who's that gentleman? Your husband?

AGNELLI *disappears off into the bedroom.*

Rosa That's my business . . . and what's this white thing? Your wife?

Man No, it's a dishwasher, for you.

Rosa For me? A dishwasher? You're mad. I never ordered a dishwasher.

Man Obviously, they've given you a present!

Rosa Me?! Who did? You can take it away with you!

Man All I know is that it's for you, and I'm not taking it back. Goodbye! (*He exits*)

Rosa Look, you're not going to force it on me . . .

Double (*From within*) What's going on now?

Rosa They've forced a dishwasher on me!

The DOUBLE *sticks his head round the door.*

Double And what's strange about that? For 80 years, we've been forcing our cars on the whole of Italy, and nobody's ever said a word.

They both exit, into the bedroom.

MUSICAL INTERLUDE

The lid of the dishwasher opens, and another AGENT-SPY *sticks his head out. The* MAN *in overalls comes back through the hall door, and dismantles the papier-mâché bust of Plutarch-Suetonius. He takes the bust over to the* AGENT *whose head is sticking out of the dishwasher. He puts the bust over his head. The* AGENT *freezes, like a statue.*

The other AGENT, *in the sideboard, takes the lid off his soup tureen, and looks over at the dishwasher, with the bust on top. Then he puts the tureen lid back on his head.*

At that moment, the television comes on: inside we see the face of the
AGENT-SPY *whom we already know. He too eyes up what's going on in*
the room. Then he switches off, and disappears into darkness. Enter
LUCIA.

Lucia Rosa, Rosa, are you in?

ROSA *enters.*

Rosa What's up?
Lucia Extraordinary news . . .!
Rosa Of Antonio?

The DOUBLE *also enters.*

Lucia No, not exactly, but indirectly. Good morning, Mr Agnelli.

The furniture is suddenly startled by the word 'AGNELLI'.

Double No! Don't call me Agnelli! I've already told you. Just Mr Gianni!
Rosa So, what's this extraordinary news, then?
Lucia It was on the radio, less than half an hour ago . . . and on television . . .
    Didn't you hear?
Rosa On television?

She goes over to the TV set and switches it on. On the screen we see the
SECRET AGENT, *who mimes a TV announcer. He opens and shuts his*
mouth like a fish, but we hear no voice.

Double No, we haven't heard anything.
Rosa The sound never works on this damn thing!

She bangs the TV on the side. It goes dead.

Double So anyway, what is the extraordinary news?
Lucia It said that Prime Minister Spadolini has received a letter supposedly from
    Agnelli.
Rosa Don't be silly . . .
Lucia Yes, and another letter has been received by Minister of the Interior,
    Rognoni . . .
Rosa Well, obviously, they must be fake letters! Where on earth is he supposed to
    have written them from?
Lucia From the Red Brigade's hideout where he's being held prisoner.
Rosa But he's here . . .
Double Yes, those letters are authentic. I wrote them!

All the bits of furniture shuffle forward a few inches to where the three are
sitting round the table, centre-stage.

Rosa and Lucia You? When?
Double Three days ago. I wrote them, and then I went down to post them.

He goes over to the telephone, and picks up a book.

Rosa But why? And what did you write in those letters?

Double Just a moment, and you can read for yourselves . . . There you are. Pages one and two.

He hands them the book.

Lucia But this is a collection of Aldo Moro's letters during the kidnap . . .

Rosa Yes, it's one of my books.

Double Precisely. In fact I found it in the other room there . . . The idea came to me as I was thumbing through it. I copied out the letters . . . with a few minor alterations. Here, look, I copied word for word the letter addressed to Cossiga[9] but instead of addressing it to Cossiga, I addressed it to Spadolini . . . Then I took the one to Rognoni . . . Rognoni was already Rognoni in Moro's[10] time . . . then he was Rognoni in Forlani's time . . . and Rognoni is still Rognoni now . . . Rognoni is always Rognoni! However, first of all, I made copies of my letters. Here they are. Obviously, I signed them, with my name.

The dishwasher moves closer to the DOUBLE, *so as to get a closer look at the signature. The other pieces of furniture also shuffle up. They form a little circle around* AGNELLI.

I don't feel very well today . . .

Lucia Rosa, what's the matter with that dishwasher? It seems to be moving of its own accord!

Rosa It must be the vibrations from the motor . . .

Lucia But it's not switched on . . .

Rosa Well, switch it on, then . . . Maybe it'll stop.

She wheels the dishwasher back to its place. The other bits of furniture also move back into position.

Lucia What are you saying? It stops when you switch it on?

Rosa But why did you send those copied letters? They'll realise immediately that they're the same as the Moro letters.

Double Yes, of course they will . . . All of them, the politicians, the ministers, the journalists . . . But they'll pretend they haven't noticed. In fact, I made one big change. I came straight to the point: I demanded an immediate exchange with political prisoners . . . in exchange for my life, 32 prisoners, all of them prisoners serving life sentences.

Rosa And my Antonio?

Double No, your husband isn't serving a life sentence . . . at least, not yet. And anyway, if we were to ask for him as well, it would imply that Antonio is an authentic terrorist. Let's not forget that everyone will be 100% convinced that I wrote these letters from the Red Brigade's hideout where I'm being held prisoner.

Rosa You did well not to mention Antonio . . . But why are you sending letters . . .? You're not a prisoner. What satisfaction are you hoping to get out of this?

Double Well, I want to find out what the government and the state think of me, what value I have, for them . . . I want to see whether the government, and the parties, will have the nerve to sacrifice me as they sacrificed Aldo Moro. I want to see whether, in my case too, they will reject any exchange even with a prisoner who was seriously ill . . . In order for me to be released, I'm asking for 32 to be set free . . . 32 political prisoners, all healthy in mind and limb! I've checked them one by one. And I want to see if they're going to order a blackout with the newspapers, like they did during the D'Urso kidnapping[11] . . . I'll go out and buy all the newspapers! Including *Peanuts* and *Teenage Romance*.

Lucia Excuse me, Mr Gianni, do you mind if I say something. This presumptuousness on your part is pretty disgusting. Just who do you think you are?

Double I am Gianni Agnelli!! Two hundred and seventy five factories in Europe alone . . .! Of which four are in Poland . . . In Poland . . . with those troublesome workers . . .! But I sorted them out straight away! I put one of my trusted foremen in charge . . . a certain Mr Jaruzelski . . .

Lucia So, you're hoping to take advantage of the protection offered by your prestige and your power. You have copied Moro's letters, but it's not going to do any good. Tomorrow, the journalists and the politicians in their turn will simply copy out the same replies that they gave at the time of Moro, when he asked them.

Double That remains to be seen!

Rosa She's absolutely right. I can see the headlines already: 'The State Must Make a Show of Strength by Sacrificing one of its Most Outstanding Citizens' . . .

Double Who wrote that?

Rosa Leo Valiani,[12] life senator, in *Corriere della Sera* . . . writing about Moro. From that day onwards, they now call him 'death senator'!

Double Anyway, supposing they do perform as you suggest, I have my reply ready. My last will and testament!

He pulls a sheet of paper out of his pocket.

Rosa Your will!

Double Yes, exactly; my will. I shall read it to you. 'Dear friends, gentlemen of the government, with my death, you are all sacked! At my funeral, I want nobody to be present, no government representatives, nobody from the State. I want no priest, and nobody from my family, in particular my rather stupid younger brother. I wish to be cremated. My ashes are to be taken in a helicopter, which will fly over Turin, scattering them in handfuls over the Rivalta, Spa Stura and Mirafiori factories . . . So that the workers, when they breathe, will cough, and will remember me. I may not stay in their hearts . . . but I shall remain in their lungs. For ever!'

ROSA *and* LUCIA *spit in unison.*

Enter the POLICE INSPECTOR, *with his customary insolence, accompanied by a* POLICE OFFICER.

Meanwhile the AGENT-SPY *who hid under the table, extends the table-top by a couple of feet, leaving a gap in the middle. Through this gap, the* AGENT-SPY *sticks his head. He takes the wig off the wig-stand on the table, and puts it on his own head, thereby turning himself into a wigstand.*

Inspector Good afternoon. Not disturbing you, am I?

Rosa No! I'm very happy to see you, Inspector, so that, at last, I can see my husband and find out how he is!

Inspector Unfortunately, your Antonio isn't too well. He's feeling a bit swollen . . . Partly because he keeps tripping up, and having bad falls . . .

Rosa Onto your fists, eh?

Lucia Shut up, Rosa, don't fall for it.

Inspector And partly because he keeps drinking like a fish.

Rosa But how can that be? He's almost teetotal!

Inspector True enough. It was only water he was drinking, with a bit of salt.

Rosa Water and salt?

Inspector Yes, by the gallon, down a rubber tube. You should see what a guzzleguts he is!

Rosa You rotten, horrible, stinking, pigging bastards. Torturing . . .

Inspector Now, language!

He goes to lean on the table, but it suddenly shifts out of the way, moved by the SECRET AGENT *underneath.*

What's going on?

Lucia Don't pay any attention, Inspector. You must understand . . .

Inspector Indeed I do understand. I am very understanding, as you can see from the fact that I've taken the trouble to bring your fellow up here. Get a move on, there! (*To* ROSA) Your fellow, so that you can persuade him to tell the truth!

He bangs his fist down twice on the table, as if to underline what he is saying. The third time, the table suddenly shifts out of the way.

What's going on here?

Rosa I don't know, Inspector. This has been going on all day, with the furniture moving round of its own accord . . . It must be the vibrations from the subway . . .

Inspector Anyway, up until now . . . your husband has spun us a load of cock and bull. He even went so far as to say that you, Mrs Berardi, are the person responsible for logistical operations in the Red Brigades, and that you have got Mr Agnelli hidden here . . .

The DOUBLE *pokes his head out of the fridge.*

Double Please, don't give me away!
Inspector Oi, you! Will you get a move-on?
Rosa My Antonio said that? About me?
Lucia Obviously, since they'd filled him with water, they could make him say anything they wanted!
Inspector (*Looking out of the door*) Will you get your finger out?!
Policeman We're not going to make it, Inspector. He keeps falling down, and taking us with him!
Inspector Well haul him up with a rope, then. Wait – I'll come down. You, come with me.

The INSPECTOR *and the* POLICEMAN *leave the stage.*

Rosa They're killing him.

The DOUBLE *pokes his head out again.*

Double Listen – our only way out is not to contradict him. In fact, give him as much leeway as possible. You must tell him the biggest load of nonsense you can think of . . . Fill him up with ridiculous stories. Otherwise he'll drown you like he did with Antonio. He's a raving loony!
Rosa What do you mean? Tell him that, yes, I really am in charge of logistics for the Red Brigades?
Double You must give him fibs, stories . . . you must give me time . . . We're going to spring a trap that I've set up, which will save all of us . . .
Rosa But I'm incapable of telling lies . . .
Double Pretend you're a journalist from *The Sun.* Be inventive – make it all up! Look out, they're coming back.

The DOUBLE *gets back into the fridge.*

Enter the INSPECTOR, *with the* POLICEMEN.

Inspector One more flight, and your husband will be here.
Rosa Yes, and I could spit in his eye! I knew that cretin wasn't to be trusted. He's sung like a canary!
Inspector What . . . he's sung, has he?! So there was some truth in what the cretin said!
Rosa Yes, too right! I'm going to talk. Talk, talk! I'll talk . . . and soon I'm going to repent, too. Up until yesterday, I knew where Agnelli was.
Inspector Oh yes? Where?
Rosa In an airship, a balloon, you know, the one that advertises condoms and contraceptives over the city.

Inspector What? A contraceptive dirigible?! See here, Mrs Berardi, look me in the eye.

Rosa Which one?

Inspector Don't try to make a fool of me, because there's a water pipe ready for you as well!

Out of the fridge, a shoe is passed to LUCIA, *who then hands it on to* ROSA.

Rosa Nobody's fooling here. Just for a start, here's the first evidence. (*She puts the shoe on the table*)

Inspector What's that?

Rosa Can't you see? It's a shoe. Agnelli's shoe.

Inspector Still fooling about, eh? (*He takes the shoe and examines it closely*)

Rosa Not at all: size forty-four and three quarters, hand-made, by Lenzuer Brothers, London . . .

Lucia They're specially made for him!

Rosa If you don't believe it, phone the Agnelli family and ask if it matches.

Inspector I don't need to. (*He instructs the* POLICEMAN) Call HQ.

The POLICEMAN *goes over to the telephone and lifts the receiver.*

Inspector No, not on the telephone, on the radio. They've got all his details there. Check with the clothing department.

The POLICEMAN *switches on a portable radio. Suddenly we see aerials sprouting from all the bits of furniture. Enter* ANTONIO, *accompanied by another* POLICEMAN. *His belly is swollen. As soon as he enters, he sprays water everywhere – even from his ears, if possible.*

Policeman Hello, HQ . . .?

Rosa There's the stool pigeon! We'll fix you, you rat!

Lucia Please, don't be so severe!

Antonio But Rosa . . . Glug, glug . . . (*He begins to gargle*)

Rosa Shut up, slobberer! You've ruined everything, damn traitor!

Inspector Good God! And to think that I took her for a fool.

Antonio Rosa, I'm sorry, but they filled me with . . . ooooh . . . water.

With the sponge trick, he fills his mouth with water and squirts it in the POLICEMAN'*s face.*

Inspector Take him into the toilet! Otherwise he'll drown us all!

Policeman Inspector, HQ tell me that the make, the type and the size match . . . Agnelli was the only person to wear that kind of shoe in Italy. Him and the Pope.

Inspector Good God! (*He grabs the shoe*) Let's have a photo immediately . . .

Rosa Oh yes, all of us together, round the shoe!

They form up in a 'Family photograph' group, around the shoe. One of the

POLICEMEN *pulls out a flash camera. The* SECRET AGENTS *also jump out of their bits of furniture, and blast off with their flash cameras.*

Inspector What is this? A day outing to Clacton?

Rosa So, now will you believe that we're not talking nonsense?

Inspector Yes, true, it is evidence . . . but fairly, how can I say, relative.

Lucia What do you mean, relative?

Inspector Well, one of Agnelli's shoes does not prove that you have got Agnelli himself.

Rosa What about two shoes?

> *She takes the other shoe, which the* DOUBLE *has passed to* LUCIA, *and bangs it down on the table. Once again, the* SECRET AGENTS *loose off with their flash cameras.*

Inspector Well, yes, two shoes . . .

Rosa And that's not the end of it . . .

> *She pulls a sheet of paper out of one of the shoes.*

Inspector Three shoes?

Rosa No, the original carbon copies of the letters to Spadolini and Rognoni, written in Agnelli's own hand.

> *She hands the sheet to the* INSPECTOR.

Inspector The copies? Are you sure? Watch out, because if this is a joke, it could cost you dearly.

> *All the furniture comes shuffling up to the* INSPECTOR *and* ROSA.

Rosa It could cost you even dearer, my dear Inspector, if you don't hurry up and carry out the necessary handwriting examination.

Inspector Get a move on, run down to HQ.

Policeman Yes, I'm running. (*He bumps into the coat rack*) Oh, excuse me!

Agent-Spy Don't mention it.

Policeman Wait a minute, Inspector, I've got the evening edition of two newspapers: this one's got the letter sent to Spadolini. It's an enlarged reprint.

> *The* INSPECTOR *compares the copy with the newspaper.*

Inspector Well, yes, the handwriting is very clear, and it looks pretty much the same . . .

> *In order to get a better view, the furniture begins to take things to excess, climbing up on the table, leaning up against the group of* POLICEMEN, *forming a kind of pyramid.*

But don't keep pushing!

Policeman It's not me, Inspector, it's the table, the hat stand, the T.V. and the sideboard!

The pieces of furniture slowly disentangle themselves from the pile, and go back to their original positions.

Inspector That ruddy subway really is playing up!

The window whizzes out from the wings, and stops in front of the group standing centre-stage.

Inspector I need a magnifying glass . . .

Rosa I've got one in the drawer . . .

She goes over the sideboard, and goes to open a drawer. A hand comes out of the tureen and hands ROSA a magnifying-glass.

Ah, no, it was in the tureen!

She hands the glass to the INSPECTOR.

There you are, it's got a little light built in, too.

The SECRET AGENT standing behind the coat rack shines a big torch on the newspaper.

Inspector Good Lord, what a powerful light (*He examines the letter and newspaper closely*) It looks like a pretty good forgery to me.

Lucia What do you mean, a forgery. Who could have done it? Nobody has ever seen a single line written by Agnelli up until now. And this newspaper only came out an hour ago!

Policeman it looks pretty authentic to me too.

Rosa Right, that'll do!

She snatches the sheet of paper from the POLICEMAN and runs off. She gives the paper to LUCIA. Everyone chases after ROSA, who disappears behind the coat rack.

All the pieces of furniture start a merry-go-round. Lights flash on and off. The music gets louder. Shouting and laughter, as at a funfair.

Inspector Stop it! My head's spinning . . .!

Suddenly everything returns to normal, and the furniture returns to its original position.

Inspector You're nicked. Talk! Where have you stashed Mr Agnelli?

Rosa I will only talk if I'm free, and only if I have Crown witness immunity, repentant terrorist, special category, supergrass status.

Lucia That's right, without immunity you won't talk!

Inspector You'll talk or I'll blow your brains out!

Rosa Alright, I'll talk . . . But only in front of an Examining Magistrate.

Inspector He's coming. I've sent for him. You know the Examining Magistrate I mean – the one who was here last time.

Rosa Ah yes, that poor fellow whose leg you shot.

Inspector Sssh! Please!

Rosa Alright, let's wait.

Inspector No, here nobody is waiting, understand! Because I'll kill you!

> *The* INSPECTOR *pulls out a pistol, and points it at* ROSA, *who hides behind the table. Everybody dives for cover. The* SECRET AGENTS *also disappear into their respective pieces of furniture, like snails into their shells.*

Rosa Inspector, don't shoot . . . I'm not a car at a road block! Don't shoot. Alright, I'll talk . . .

Inspector Oh, so you've finally come to your senses. Listen here, from now on, I'm not going to ask you questions . . . You're going to talk loud and long, and God help anyone who interrupts! (*Turning to the two* POLICEMEN) Incidentally, is our swollen friend still in the toilet?

Policeman Yes, Sir, I locked him in . . .

Inspector Well done. Go and take a look at him.

> *Exit the* POLICEMAN. *He returns after a moment.*

Alright, get on with it. Be precise, and keep to the point: when did you first decide to kidnap Agnelli? (*To the two* POLICEMEN) You write, and you record.

> *The* DOUBLE *begins to feed* ROSA *ideas from out of the fridge.*

Rosa The idea of kidnapping Agnelli was formulated at about the time when we were preparing the via Fani operation[13] . . .

> *The furniture shuffles slowly closer, so as to hear* ROSA'*s story.*

Inspector I want details, names, dates, addresses, everything!

Rosa The story begins in early January . . . 1978 . . . I was in Milan. It was a lovely day. A pale sun shone weakly through the mist that hung over the city . . .

Inspector Never mind the hazy sun and the mist . . . This is a verbal, not fucking Shakespeare . . .

Rosa (*To the* DOUBLE) See, you're making a fool of me! Alright, no poetry. The strategic meeting to discuss kidnapping Agnelli took place in a . . . cinema!

> *This last phrase came out of its own accord. Spontaneously, with no prompting from the* DOUBLE, *the* INSPECTOR *is bewildered. He slowly comes over to her. The* DOUBLE *retreats into the fridge.*

Inspector In a cinema? A strategic meeting in a cinema?

> ROSA *looks towards the fridge, seeking help. She pushes her seat towards it, in an attempt to get closer. Then she gives up, and carries on, regardless. With vigour:*

Rosa Yes! The Astoria . . . a nice little cinema, near my house . . . So we have our meetings there, because of my feet . . . And . . . when they called the meeting, I was sitting in Piazzo del Duomo, with my girlfriend Caterina . . .

Inspector Who is Caterina?

Rosa He's a priest . . .

Inspector A priest? There's a priest involved too?

> LUCIA, *worried by the enormity of it all, starts signalling desperately to stop.*

> ROSA, *unperturbed, warms to her theme.*

Rosa Yes . . . Don Anselmo . . . a worker priest from Canegrate.[14] He's infiltrated the church establishment.

Inspector And he dresses up as a woman?

Rosa Yes. He looks great in drag. He's really elegant, with high heels, lovely perfume and long, wavy hair.

Inspector Does he wear a wig?

Rosa No wig. Just his own natural hair. It's very long . . . and when he goes back to being a priest, he gathers it in a bun, like so, and tucks it under his hat.

Inspector And his titties . . .? Presumably they're his own as well, presumably they're also *au naturel*?

Rosa No, he always keeps two lightweight hand grenades in his bra: for tactical use! We call him Brother Boob Bomb.

Inspector But this is out of this world! Listen, you're not making all this up . . .?

Rosa Well, all you have to do is phone the Vatican, ask for Don Anselmo . . . and when a woman's voice answers . . . Bob's your uncle.

Policeman Hello . . . is that the Archbishop's office?

Rosa Oh, come on Inspector. You know very well, repentant terrorists never lie! Alright, so there we were, in the Astoria . . . They were showing a porn film . . . the story of a sex-mad police inspector, who falls in love with a transvestite, and who, in the end, turns homosexual himself . . . He ends up soliciting in the park . . . gets caught in a police round-up. They take him down to the police station, where he's beaten up by the police chief . . . a known sadist, who beats him almost to death. The sex-mad transvestite inspector is about to breathe his last, when the police chief is suddenly seized with passion and shouts: 'Don't breathe your last . . . I love you!!' They marry and live happily ever after. Nice story, eh?

Inspector Hmm . . . Continue, please!

Rosa Yes, let's continue. So there we are, watching the film, when the doors of the cinema swing open, and who should come in but the lawyer for . . . Mr Big!

Inspector No!!

Lucia Rosa, no!

Inspector Mr Big! So he really does exist, then! Who is he?

Rosa My friend Lucia is right, at this point I don't think I can continue . . . From now on, we're dealing with names, places and people who are too important . . . I can't go on.

Inspector Still fooling about eh?

Rosa No, Inspector, I am not starting tricks. Even the President of the Republic, Pertini, on 31st December, 1981, when he made his New Year speech to the people of Italy, made a clear reference to terrorism and its bases . . . which, he said, were not in Italy, but abroad, in Europe as a whole . . .

Inspector Ah, yes . . . when he spoke about international connections . . .

Rosa Yes, international. So, if the President of the Italian Republic, with all the protection that he has, and the knowledge that he has . . . limits himself only to a passing reference . . . and did not name names . . . he, who could . . . he, who knows . . . and you, a humble Inspector . . . Please don't get me wrong . . . want to play at Don Quixote . . . want to risk your own life by knowing too much! Do you actually want to die? Well, if you want to die, then why should I stop you, Inspector? After everything that you've done to my family . . . to my husband . . . No, I shall tell you the names. (*To one of the* POLICEMEN) Are you ready to record this, for the 'last' time. (*To the other* POLICEMAN) Are you ready to write this down for the 'last' time? (*To the* INSPECTOR) Are you ready to listen, for the 'last' time?

Lucia Rosa, if you're going to talk, then I'm going . . . I don't fancy dying.

LUCIA *exits.*

1st Policeman Excuse me, Inspector, I've got to go too . . .

Inspector Go where?

1st Policeman My shift's over, and also my wife is ill. I have to take her to the hospital . . .

2nd Policeman I've got to go too, Inspector . . . I've got an abscess come up on a tooth, and I've got to go and have my gum lanced . . .

Inspector You're a bunch of rotten cowards! The abscess is not on your gums . . . it's up your arses!

Exit the two POLICEMEN, *followed by all the furniture.*

Rosa Inspector . . . my furniture . . . It's moving of its own accord! Stop it . . .(*She shouts after the fleeing furniture*) Come back . . .! Come back!

Inspector (*His hand goes to his heart*) Oh God, I feel ill . . . my heart . . .

He slumps down in a chair.

Rosa Are you feeling ill? You see what happens when you try to find out too much? (*She runs to the hall door and shouts*) Lucia . . . Officers . . . Hurry up . . . the Inspector is ill!

Re-enter LUCIA, *followed by the* POLICEMEN.

Lucia What's happening?

Enter a POLICE OFFICER *with newspapers.*

Policeman Look Guv, I've got the special editions. What's in them is unbelievable!

Slowly all the pieces of furniture come back on-stage, and line up behind the actors. The fridge opens, and out pops the DOUBLE.

Double Pass me one too. (*The* POLICEMAN *passes him a newspaper*) Thank you.

Policeman Hey, but that's the prisoner, what's he doing in there?

Double Just keeping cool . . . Listen, the whole Cabinet has met and issued a communiqué. Here it is, under the headline: 'Kidnap Chaos. Cabinet Caves In. Yes. In the Moro Case, the State Answered: No Exchange. This Time it Must Answer: Yes'.

All in Unison No!

Double No, yes 'The prisoners asked for in exchange, will be set free today.'

All in Unison Oh no!

Double Yes. 'We are aware that after the 32 prisoners have been released, Agnelli's jailers demand the release of an unlimited number of further prisoners, in order to prevent this . . .'

All in Unison Well?

Double 'The Cabinet, with the approval of the various organs of state, has decided to free all political prisoners already serving sentences.'

All in Unison No!

Double Yes! 'And also all prisoners awaiting trial'.

Lucia Evviva!

Rosa Evviva! So my Antonio is free!!

Lucia Yes, everyone's free!

Inspector No, it's impossible, have they all gone mad?

Double Sorry, Inspector. 'All anti-terrorist proceedings have been dropped as well.' You can retire peacefully.

Inspector All the work that I've done, my hard work, flushed down the pan! It's disgusting! Bastard politicians!

The furniture standing behind the actors also begins to get agitated.

Rosa Bastard politicians is right. They let Moro be killed like a lamb led to the slaughter: everyone agreed that he should be sacrificed. Be firm! And now, with Agnelli, they've done a somersault. The loathsome pigs!

Lucia Yes, all of them with their trousers down, giving in like crazy!

They look at each other in amazement.

Double You don't understand? Tell me, have you never read Karl Marx? Ah yes, of course . . . These days only we captains of industry study *Das Kapital* . . . Especially where it says: 'The only true power is financial-economic power, in other words, holding companies, markets, banks, commodities, in other words, Capital.'

One of the POLICEMEN *leaves the stage by the centre door.*

And then he adds a sentence, which children should memorise and sing in the playground: 'The sacred laws of this state . . . the economic state . . . are written on watermarked paper money. So government, state and institutions are nothing other than supporting services, for the real power, which is economic power.' Supporting services . . . you see? So, Aldo Moro was sacrificed in order to save the respectability of the aforementioned financial state, not for the supporting services for which nobody gives a damn! Get it into your heads: I am the state! The capital which I represent is the state! It is my dignity that you must preserve, even at the cost of your own lives! How could they think of sacrificing me, in order to save the state. For I am the state.

Inspector What's he saying now? Who's he talking about? Has he gone silly in the head again? Who do you think you've turned into this time?

Double *(Reaching the top of the pile of furniture)* I am Gianni Agnelli! And don't be fooled by my face, it's because of plastic surgery . . .

Inspector Listen, I'll give you plastic surgery if you don't stop . . .

Rosa Calm down, Inspector, he really is Agnelli.

The POLICEMAN *enters.*

Policeman Inspector, in the toilet there's another Antonio, the spitting image of this one . . .

Rosa Yes, only that one is my Antonio, and this one is Agnelli.

The SECRET AGENTS *emerge from their various pieces of furniture. In chorus:*

Secret Agents Yes, Inspector, we can assure you, we have been listening in on their conversations for quite some while.

Inspector *(Pointing to the* AGENTS) Just a minute: SISMI, SISDE, Interpol, SAS, DHSS . . .

Group Leader It seems that this gentleman really is Mr Agnelli, and that, by mistake, his face has been rebuilt in the image of Antonio Berardi, one of his workers. It was he who wrote the letters to the Government, and posted them from this house, pretending that he was held prisoner by terrorists: it was he who organised this whole bloody shambles . . .

As if hypnotised, the INSPECTOR *slowly climbs up the pile of furniture, approaching* AGNELLI. AGNELLI *reaches out a hand, and with his forefinger touches the forefinger of the* INSPECTOR. *This is an obvious and grotesque allusion to Michelangelo's famous 'Creation' painting in the Sistine Chapel.*

Double I created you. Go forth!

The INSPECTOR *comes down again, bewildered.*

Inspector You're having me on! You're taking the piss! I don't care if you are the upper reaches of the State! (*He pulls a gun out of his pocket*) I'll shoot this State in the bollocks!

Chorus No, stop it, you're mad! Think of what you're doing! Stop him!

> *Everyone tries to stop him. They manage to get hold of him. At that moment, enter the* EXAMINING MAGISTRATE *on crutches.*

Examining Magistrate What's up? What's going on?

> *A shot is fired from the* INSPECTOR's *gun. BANG! The* EXAMINING MAGISTRATE *is hit in the leg.*

> Aaaargh! They've kneecapped my other kneecap! This is getting to be a habit!

> *He falls flat on his face.*

MUSICAL INTERLUDE

BLACKOUT

THE END

Popular Culture

A Speech by Dario Fo*

What follows is the text of a speech given by Dario Fo at a Conference on Culture organized by La Comune at the Palazzino Liberty in Milan on 13 June 1974. Present in the audience were a number of prominent Italian and foreign artists and directors, including Bernardo Bertolucci, Ettere Scola, Mario Monicelli, the Taviani brothers, Cesare Zavattini, Umberto Eco, Bernard Dort and Jarvis Ivens.

Popular theatre has no rules or fixed models which are mechanically reproducible. We've realised through experience that every situation of struggle, every different space in which we make a theatrical contribution, requires a complete re-thinking of techniques and theatrical methods. We've carried out a number of what you could call cultural operations, but these activities have been shaped by particular situations, needs, and sometimes very dramatic deadlines. When we first went into an alternative circuit which we hoped, or rather intended, to be a real alternative, we decided we couldn't just fall back on doing 'road shows' (*'messa da campo'*). *'Messa da campo'* is jargon for putting on shows with pot-luck means, but most of all with a very rough and ready structure . . .

I'm talking about when we were still 'Nuova Scena'† and we used to put on plays in the 'Case del popolo' (Communist Party community centres). We'd turn up with a truck load of stuff, spend all day rigging up a suitable stage, and fit up 40 or 50 lights, since we felt that people are used to a certain type of writing on television and in straight theatre, when they go to it, and we had to prevent them from getting the feeling that here was someone turning up with 'ephemeral theatre', with a roadshow, a theatre which wasn't using the means which they consciously or unconsciously were used to.

This was what we were concerned with. You might say it was excessive, but it was crucial, and it had a positive effect. We put on plays in which all the actors were also technicians – they set up the play, the lights, the whole structure, together with comrades from wherever we were who'd get the message and give us a hand – this was part of a whole new way of putting on theatre. The comrades we played to soon realized that our company was completely different from bourgeois theatres, with their division of roles, where there are technicians, 'stage hands', costumists, electricians, and then in a separate category – in the dressing room – there are the actors, as it still is now in so-called progressive theatres like the Piccolo Teatro. For the audiences in the 'Case del popolo' who noticed there was no division of roles, that we were all together once we got into the theatre, right down to the last person, this was a whole new idea of culture.

* Translated by Tony Mitchell and first published in *Theater*, the magazine of the Yale School of Drama.

† When they left the 'bourgeois theatre' in 1968, the 'Campagnia Dario Fo – Franca Rame' was dissolved and became the theatre collective 'Nuova Scena'. In 1970, after an internal split in 'Nuova Scena', Dario Fo, Franca Rame and other comrades formed the 'Colletiva Teatrale – La Comune'.

The point is that it's not enough just to change venues, stop going to normal theatres, and instead of going to the Theatre Royal with its stucco and plush velvet, go to a 'Casa del popolo' – and think you've performed a revolutionary act. No chance. The first and foremost thing about being involved in this type of theatre is that you have to be a *militant* who redefines his or her relationship with the profession. It's something polemical, and I want to stress this. There are theatres which claim to be revolutionary and progressive, and still insist on this division of roles. Actors only turn up just before the play's ready to begin, go and make up, do a few voice exercises, gargle a bit, read over their part, chat about their latest exploit or the latest book they've read, or the latest crap, etc., etc., then meditate for a couple of minutes to 'get into the part', to create a spiritual state which is exactly the dimension of reactionary theatre, and finally go on stage, hoping that night they'll find the right spiritual and moral conditions from the audience to be able to do their prestigious number and play their magic theatrical card. So our 'Casa del popolo' experience was very important, but we had to go a step further than that. Once we decided to play in other places as well, completely anti-theatrical spaces like piazzas, sports stadiums, deconsecrated churches, factory prefabs, then we discovered the problem of breaking down the 'fourth wall'.

What does the 'fourth wall' mean? It's that magic moment which is determined by the proscenium arch which divides the audience from the actors. So the fourth wall is just this rectangular space? No, it's also the lighting cues which create a particular atmosphere, the footlights, the pink and orange filters on the lamps, the solidly entrenched sets and the aquarium atmosphere the actors and props are placed in, the corpse-like make up on the actors' faces, their gestures and voice projection, with its fixed cadences, sung, whispered or shouted, giving the audience the feeling of being like peeping-toms spying on a story which is totally remote from them and which is ever there on the other side of the fourth wall. It's an intimate, naturalistic, or else metaphysical conception of theatre.

So how do you break down the fourth wall? Get rid of the curtain and destroy that magic cut-off moment, and create a situation of audience participation just because you've dispensed with the curtain like the Brechtians do? No such luck. Getting rid of the curtain's not enough – what about getting rid of the stage, shifting the action into the aisles of the stalls, with the actors sitting on the audience's knees, spitting in their eyes, making them smell their sweat, hear their voices right inside their eardrums, feel uncomfortable or even comfortable – is that breaking down the fourth wall?

The bourgeois theatre has a fourth wall, that's for sure. Stanislavsky says that when actors perform they have to go about it in such a way that the audience listening to them are there *par hasard*, they just happen to be there. Actors have to get the audience to enter into a state of mind of not existing at that moment in the auditorium, and to get them to forget about the theatrical fiction, and make them feel like they're filching a story or a drama from someone else. And to reach this point you have to eliminate the 'aside'. Now what's an 'aside'? It's what you use to get the audience to participate, and it comes from popular theatre – take note, not the bourgeois theatre, because 'asides' exist in all the theatre of the sixteenth and seventeenth century theatre, like that of Lope de Vega and Goldoni, just to mention a couple of names – but this technique of the 'aside' has already been stood on its head. The 'aside' of the popular tradition is the sort of situation where the actor turns to another actor and says, 'What? You think I'm scared of you?' and then turns to the audience and says, 'Actually I'm not in the slightest bit scared, but let's hope he falls for my threats of violence,' and then says to the character, 'You know I'm perfectly ready, willing and able to stick my knife into your guts', and then to the audience, 'Let's hope he doesn't flash his dagger, or bloody hell, I'll have to scarper.' Everything that's behind his statements is expressed directly. This sort of 'aside' has been turned into a literary device, an easy way out in a certain type of bourgeois theatre.

In the beginning the 'aside' broke down the fourth wall. Now what does this mean exactly? It means that when the actor said something to another actor, he or she immediately said the opposite to the audience, and was making a 'commentary', a *criticism* from outside his or her character, detaching him or herself rationally from the character. In other words, this was epic acting. Even more importantly, when the actor addressed the audience, s/he was provoking them. In fact, the use of 'incidents' (or stage business) to create an 'aside' was fundamental in this type of theatre. What sort of 'incidents' were there in medieval theatre? One example is the expedient of having a dog come on stage or into the auditorium, running around, wagging its tail, barking, and generally causing chaos and confusion, and disrupting the action on stage. This gave the actor a pretext to start talking to the audience and break through the fourth wall, because the incident gave him or her the opportunity to step out, and break down the framework the scene was being represented in. Other incidents were a child crying, a lamp going out, or even starting a fire. One of the most famous 'asides' was by Cerea, a sixteenth-century actor, a contemporary of Ruzante's, who invented the expedient of a wasp to break down the wall. While he was performing, he started acting as if a wasp was bothering him. He was very good at buzzing like a wasp, and after a while this wasp was flying around all over the place, over the other people, all over the stage, and he was following it around. In short, he tried to involve the audience in this new grotesque situation while still carrying on with the story. Ruzante used direct dialogue with the audience as well, – he was always talking to them, constantly addressing them. But not just to achieve an aesthetic break – he needed the audience to participate in the stage action with the constant awareness that it was fiction.

And then came the split between popular culture and bourgeois culture – there's an historical example of this in Andreini's letter. Andreini was an actor who went to France in the middle of the 1500s, and was recognised all over Europe as a great actor and a great inventor of theatrical language. And what had he invented? The fourth wall, no less. He was the one who imposed this dimension. He ordered his actors not to do any more 'asides' to the audience as they used to do, but to do them directly to another character who was put there on stage specially as a feed . . . There were servants, porters, extras, characters invented just to be feeds for 'asides'. 'You have to forget that there's an audience in the auditorium – you're in a theatre, not a piazza'. This sanctioned an ideological attitude which we still find in bourgeois theatre today.

It is the exact opposite of what Brecht insisted on when he talked about acting in the third person. Now what did he mean? He meant that the actor doesn't so much act as *represent*. And what did he mean by 'represent'? He meant making continuous 'asides' – in other words, constantly talking to the audience. In order to talk to the audience about what's going on, actors have to interrupt themselves, step out of character, and act as mediators, representing and describing the character. This technique is not a merely aesthetic matter, it is the basis of a completely different, ideological vision of theatre, cinema, or expression in any art form.

But where does this other way of communicating come from, and what is it? It stems from a class culture on the one hand, and a reactionary bourgeois culture on the other. A pessimistic culture on one side, and a culture which is striving for socialism on the other. A culture which stems from a collective need for participation, or involvement. Not involvement in the sense of all that crap that lots of kids working in the theatre think it is, that involving the audience means going down among them, making them feel uncomfortable, treading on their toes, performing sprawled out over them . . . No, involvement in the rational sense of the word. Not involvement at gut level, where I examine *my* problems, *my* crises, *my* helplessness, *my* impotence, and since I'm talking about it making my confession to all these people, that makes it popular theatre. I mean involvement in terms of an all-round discussion, a vision of the world, the problem of destroying a society and building a new one. It is not a *personal* condition, meaning that I'm so much better off with other people around, because we've discovered a collective identity. This has got nothing to do with Maoism or Marxism. This sort of view is simply reverting to an individualistic standpoint.

What I'm interested in is a much more provocative field of activity. When we've reached the point where we agree we need to break down the fourth wall, we find ourselves completely opposed to the idea of identifying the actor with the character: the actor is *me*, I try to identify with him or her, and inside myself all the fripperies, the innards, all my defects, all my qualities, in an attempt to dress up the character as myself. That's what Stanislavsky's all about, and it's the worst type of reactionary, conservative, bourgeois position in history.

If instead I try to create the vision of a community, a chorus, a communion, obviously I'm not going to be too concerned about talking about myself – I'm talking about collective problems. If I seek out collective problems, what I'm saying and the language I use will be different; it'll be forced to be epic. This is why all the popular theatre is always epic, because it's based on a clear ideological fact – the ideology of community, of a communion of interests, social interests, interests of living together, producing together, and sharing the proceeds.

We've had specific experiences in this field. We've realised, for example, that it's not enough just to stage vertically disruptive plays, but that what we have to do is break down certain situations of dialogue. We've also realised that there's a good reason for the fact that the medieval actor used to perform alone on stage and develop a number of characters. This was the only means he had to establish an epic quality to his performance, and make it collective through his own continuous presence. Then something else happened, and we encountered the necessity of having to organise 'improvised' shows, which is a way of doing theatre that we used to despise, because we thought it was ephemeral. Then we realised it was 'ephemeral', not in terms of the point being made, but in terms of quality. To put it briefly, the 'roadshows' we were talking about before, and their poverty of means, are just a question of ideological attitude. This was because previously we hadn't discovered a model, a form, a precise language with which we could put on this type of show as professionals and not as amateurs. It couldn't be makeshift, there couldn't be anything smacking of, 'Well, we couldn't do any better than that' – it had to be art, in the sense of the art of direct intervention.

We realised that our recent experiences had given us the courage to overturn the rules of a theatre which has always been looked upon like the Parthenon. The courage as aware professionals to improvise, to put together a play in 24 hours and take it to a trial, to go to a trial in the morning and then summarise what had happened in the trial in theatrical form, in a grotesque, critical form of theatre with songs, in four hours . . .

Sure, there wasn't any aesthetic structure, there wasn't any of that wonderful balance of planned and rehearsed voices, lights, timing and punchlines – there was very little at all of what you could put down to the balance of 'good theatre'. It was carved out with a hatchet, but in fact that was all to the good, according to some comrades who were there, and found the play useful as a sounding board for their political work. They said, 'Let's have more of these shows,' even if they are scrappy. And they were scrappy – we were the first to be unhappy about them. The comrades in the audience who went to the more dramatic performance put on by the state the next day were able to make a comparison and realise the truth about the justice and the fascism in the whole event.

Obviously, if you carry on doing this form of theatre, and you have the opportunity to develop in this direction, you'll produce much better things. But it doesn't matter if the results are sometimes modest, it's a whole new experience, even if it is an experience which has caused a decline in our work on a production level, in terms of 'finished products'. And then you tell me, 'You've really reached rock bottom in technique and art.' Maybe we have, but at a political level, at the level of developing the ideological and cultural dimension of our work, I think we've made progress. We can think about art later.

NOTES

1. Agnelli, head of the Fiat Motor Corporation, Chairman of Confindustria, the equivalent of the BFI. International financier. A powerful political force in Italy aiming at a 'strong state'.
2. A famous old-established Italian circus.
3. The Communist Party daily newspaper.
4. One of the main Fiat plants in Turin.
5. Christian Democrat politician; has held many offices including that of Prime Minister.
6. Members of terrorist groups who became 'supergrasses'.
7. Greek and Roman historians.
8. A right-wing bombing in Brescia in Northern Italy which caused a number of deaths.
9. Christian Democrat politician, Prime Minister at the time of the kidnapping of Moro, the Christian Democrat chairman who was one of the chief architects of the 'historic compromise' with the Communist Party, which thus for the first time since the war was part of the Italian government.
10. Christian Democrat politicians who held various posts in successive coalitions; they formed part of what Pasolini the writer and film-maker, called 'the Palace' – the centre of political power in Italy.
11. An examining magistrate who was kidnapped but freed after negotiations with the terrorists.
12. Senator for life, who had a distinguished Resistance record; advocated the use of the death penalty for terrorism.
13. Scene of a right-wing terrorist attack.
14. An industrial area of Milan.

ACCIDENTAL DEATH OF AN ANARCHIST
DARIO FO
Adapted by Gavin Richards

Running for over two years at the Wyndhams
Theatre, London, this put Fo's work on the
map in Britain.
  Hilarious, caustic satire on police corruption
in Italy. Fo at his best.

  'Loud, vulgar, kinetic, scurrilous, smart,
sensational show.' *New Society*

51 pages
0 86104 217 4   £1.50 paperback

CAN'T PAY? WON'T PAY!
DARIO FO

A major success in London's West End in 1981/82 at the Criterion Theatre, this is a political farce about a strike by Italian housewives against price rises.

'Anarchy, theft, class war and bopping the fuzz . . . it is like a shotgun marriage between Feydeau and Proudhon . . . a play that extracts whooping laughter from social injustice.' *Guardian*
'A rare tribute to the resourceful powers of laughter.' *Times*

72 pages
0 86104 222 0   £2.50 paperback

FEMALE PARTS
ONE WOMAN PLAYS
DARIO FO and FRANCA RAME

In *Waking Up*, a young woman reconstructs
the various phases of her day. She shows that
she is trapped — by her husband, her baby,
her work and her home.

In *A Woman Alone*, a housewife is locked
up at home by her possessive husband — a
paradoxical and comic interpretation of a
woman used as a sexual object.

The Same Old Story is a hilariously
scatalogical fairy tale about a sexual
relationship.

In the fourth play, *Medea*, Medea kills her
own children in the painful awareness that
children are the links of a chain which society
hangs round the necks of women, 'like a heavy
wooden yoke that makes us easier to milk and
easier to mount'.

Translated from the Italian, *Female Parts:
One Woman Plays*, is now in repertory at the
National Theatre, London.

'Rude, raucous and funny . . . This is high-
grade, feminist farce about a woman always
on her feet.' Michael Billington, *Guardian*

48 pages
0 86104 220 4   £2.50 paperback

CLOUD NINE
CARYL CHURCHILL

Cloud Nine is an inventive, surrealistic and entertaining look at sexual repression and sexual role conditioning. It has been highly successful on the stage in both London and New York.

    Cloud Nine shows the sexual confusion — uproarious and pathetic — that besets its characters: first in colonial Africa and then, a century later, in the changing sexuality of our own times.

64 pages
0 86104 223 9   £2.50 paperback
Not for sale in the USA

BALL BOYS
DAVID EDGAR

Class struggle on the lawn tennis courts, or rather behind the scenes, by the author of the anti-fascist play *Destiny*.

32 pages
0 86104 202 6   £1.25 paperback

FEMALE TRANSPORT
STEVE GOOCH

A stark, hard-hitting account of the political
education of six women, convicted of petty
crimes in 19th century London and sentenced
to hard labour in Australia. Throughout the
six-month voyage, the cramped, below-deck
cell teaches them certain rough truths about
society.
   The women's development is powerfully
and sympathetically portrayed.

'A tough, realistic and detailed account of
the hardships endured by six female convicts
transported to Australia in the early 19th
century.' Michael Billington, *The Guardian*

72 pages
0 902818 62 7   £2.95 paperback

THE WOMEN PIRATES
ANN BONNEY AND MARY READ
STEVE GOOCH

About two women at the turn of the 18th
century who joined a rebel pirate community
in the Caribbean.

84 pages
0 904383 86 5   £2.50 paperback

APRICOTS and THERMIDOR
TREVOR GRIFFITHS

Two short plays: *Apricots* is a lyrical erotic
interlude on love, and *Thermidor* on the
lingering Stalinism and lack of thaw in Russia.

24 pages
0 86104 206 9   £1.00 paperback

THE CHERRY ORCHARD
ANTON CHEKHOV
Translated by Trevor Griffiths

The Cherry Orchard was Chekhov's last play.
Written in 1904 it was also the first of his plays
to reflect the stirrings of the Russian people
inside the prison of Czarist despotism.

'The translation is lithe, speakable and
humourous.' *New Statesman*

96 pages
0 904383 73 3   £2.50 paperback

LITTLE RED HEN
JOHN MCGRATH

Fifty years of Scottish labour history as told by
the old grannie hen to her young SNP hen
granddaughter.

64 pages
0 904383 31 8   £2.50 paperback

TAKING OUR TIME
RED LADDER

A 'socio-historical documentary' on the mid-
19th-century Chartist movement in the
industrial Midlands, by one of Britain's
foremost socialist theatre collectives.

72 pages
0 86104 210 7   £2.50 paperback

ASHES
DAVID RUDKIN

Parallels the personal dilemma of a married
couple, whose attempts at procreation are
frustrated by sterility with the public, political
dilemma of Northern Ireland.

52 pages
0 86104 208 5   £2.50 paperback

THE LORENZACCIO STORY
PAUL THOMPSON

A re-telling of Alfred de Musset's play of 1883,
showing the assassination of the Duke of
Florence to have been the abortive, isolated
statement of a single individual.

72 pages
0 904383 85 7   £2.50 paperback

THE GLAD HAND
SNOO WILSON

A wild and weirdly imaginative play which
fuses psycho-sexual fantasy with social
comment, as a ship of fools captained by a
mad South African attempts to raise the Anti-
Christ.

72 pages
0 86104 212 3   £2.50 paperback